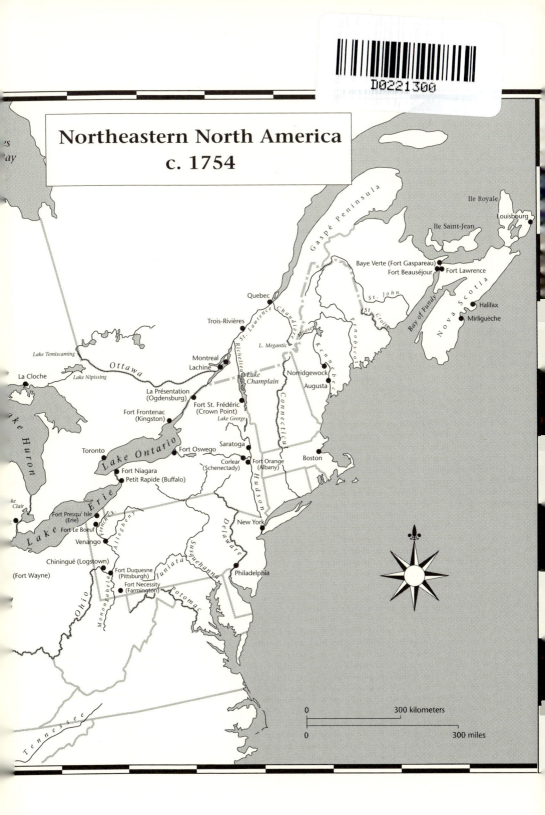

Northeastern North America
c. 1754

Ile Royale

Louisbourg

Ile Saint-Jean

Gaspé Peninsula

Baye Verte (Fort Gaspareau)
Fort Beauséjour   Fort Lawrence

Halifax

Nova Scotia

Mirliguèche

Bay of Fundy

St. John

St. Croix

Penobscot

Kennebec

Quebec

Trois-Rivières

St. Lawrence

Chaudière

Moose

L. Megantic

Norridgewock

Augusta

Connecticut

Lake Temiscaming

Ottawa

Lake Nipissing

La Cloche

Montreal
Lachine

Richelieu

Lake Champlain

La Présentation
(Ogdensburg)

Fort Frontenac
(Kingston)

Fort St. Frédéric
(Crown Point)

Lake George

Saratoga

Lake Huron

Toronto

Lake Ontario

Fort Oswego

Corlear
(Schenectady)

Fort Orange
(Albany)

Boston

Fort Niagara

Petit Rapide (Buffalo)

Lake Erie

Fort Presqu' Isle
(Erie)

Fort Le Boeuf

French Ck.

Allegheny

Hudson

New York

Delaware

Lake Clair

Venango

Chiningué (Logstown)

(Fort Wayne)

Ohio

Monongahela

Fort Duquesne
(Pittsburgh)

Fort Necessity
(Farmington)

Juniata

Susquehanna

Philadelphia

Potomac

Tennessee

ay

es

0   300 kilometers

0   300 miles

ON THE EVE OF THE CONQUEST

ON THE EVE OF THE CONQUEST

THE CHEVALIER DE RAYMOND'S CRITIQUE OF NEW FRANCE IN 1754

JOSEPH L. PEYSER

Editor and Translator

Michigan State University Press

Mackinac State Historic Parks

East Lansing/Mackinac Island

All Michigan State University Press Books are produced on paper which meets
the requirements of American National Standard of Information Sciences—
Permanence of paper for printed materials ANSI Z39.48-1984.

Michigan State University Press
East Lansing, Michigan 48823-5202

04 03 02 01 00 99 98 97   1 2 3 4 4 5 6 7 8 9

Library of Congress Cataloging-in-Publication Data

Raymond, Charles de, d. 1774
    [Dénombrement de tous les postes du Canada. English]
    On the eve of the conquest : the Chevalier de Raymond's critique of
New France in 1754 / Joseph L. Peyser, editor and translator.
        p.   cm.
    Includes bibliographical references and index.
    ISBN 0-87013-433-7
    1. New France—Politics and government. 2. Political corruption—New
France—History—18th century. 3. New France—Economic conditions.
4. France—Colonies—America—Administration—History—18th Century.
5. Trading posts—New France—History—18th Century. 6. Indians of
North America—Government relations—To 1789. 7. Raymond, Charles
de, d. 1774. I. Peyser, Joseph L., 1925-   . II. Title.
F1030.9.R3913   1997
971.01'8—dc21   97-34837
                                                                    CIP

This book has been supported by a grant [No. RL-22100-94] from the
National Endowment for the Humanities, an independent Federal Agency.

CONTENTS

MAPS

Illustrations

FOREWORD

Mackinac State Historic Parks and Indiana University South Bend jointly began the French Michilimackinac Research Project in 1991. Since then Dr. Joseph L. Peyser, Professor Emeritus of French at the university, has located thousands of French documents pertaining to Michilimackinac and the western Great Lakes and translated hundreds of them into English.

A grant from the National Endowment for the Humanities made possible the translations for this book. Generous multiyear support from the Florence Gould Foundation and our Mackinac Associates membership organization made this publication possible, and is allowing us to continue the research. The support of Chairman Dennis O. Cawthorne and the commissioners of the Mackinac Island State Park Commission provided the resources to produce this book with Michigan State University Press. We extend sincere thanks to Professor Peyser, Dr. Keith R. Widder who served as project director for Mackinac State Historic Parks, and all who contributed to the effort.

In October 1994, Professor Peyser traveled to the archives of the Séminaire de Saint-Sulpice in Paris to work with the original manuscript copy of Charles de Raymond's *dénombrement de tous les postes du Canada*. Upon his return he translated and annotated the document, which forms the core of this volume.

Mackinac State Historic Parks is pleased to issue *On the Eve of The Conquest: The Chevalier de Raymond's Critique of New France in 1754*. This follows publication in 1996 of the first book of the project, *Jacques Legardeur de Saint-Pierre: Officer, Gentleman, Entrepreneur*, also translated and edited by Professor Peyser.

With this volume Mackinac State Historic Parks continues a long tradition of making the results of historical and archaeological research available to the public. For forty years Mackinac State Historic Parks has published scholarly and popular reports, articles, and books interpreting three centuries of Straits of Mackinac history, with special attention to the historic sites we operate at Colonial Michilimackinac in Mackinaw City, Historic Mill Creek near Mackinaw City, and Fort Mackinac on Mackinac Island. The translation of Captain Raymond's assessment of New France on the eve of the French and Indian War makes a welcome addition to knowledge of the early role of the French in North American history, and of the importance of the place called Michilimackinac to national history and international commerce.

Carl R. Nold
Director, Mackinac State Historic Parks
Mackinac Island State Park Commission

ACKNOWLEDGMENTS

I am grateful to the organizations and institutions identified in the foreword of this book for having provided the funds needed for the translation, editing, annotation and publication of Charles de Raymond's *dénombrement*. Among the many individuals in these and other institutions who facilitated my work are the following: Keith R. Widder, Curator of History of the Mackinac State Historic Parks, whose outstanding editorial and collegial suggestions were invaluable to me; Irénée Noye, archivist at the Séminaire de Saint-Sulpice, Paris, whose friendly cooperation by correspondence and in person in Paris made my work at the Séminaire a pleasure; and Hélène Charlebois-Dumais, *historienne consultante* of LaSalle, Quebec, whose diligent searches in the Montreal-area archives produced valuable manuscripts and illustrations for this book, including a previously long-forgotten portrait of Abbé François Picquet.

The following also contributed importantly to this project: Laurent Tailleur, *ptre*, archivist, Musée de la civilisation, Archives du Séminaire de Québec; Eva Major-Marothy, Art Acquisition and Research Archivist, National Archives of Canada; Pauleena MacDougall, Associate Director, Maine Folklore Center, University of Maine; René Chartrand, Parks Canada (retired); Edward Dahl, Cartographic and Architectural Archives, National Archives of Canada; Marcel Demers, p.s.s., curé de la Paroisse de l'Annonciation, Oka, Quebec and Jacques Leduc, prêtre de Saint-Sulpice, Montreal, whose research located and confirmed the portrait of Abbé Picquet; Brian Leigh Dunnigan, Curator of Maps, William L. Clements Library, University of Michigan; James Pritchard, Professor of History, Queen's University; Jane S. Clark, Interpretation Supervisor, Fort Necessity National Battlefield; A.J.B. Johnston, Fortress of Louisbourg National Historic Site; Serge Courville, Professeur de géographie historique, Université Laval; Monique La Grenade-Meunier, *historienne consultante*, Saint-Lambert, Quebec; Lewis Parker, artist, Sunderland, Ontario; and William H. Fritz, Mackinac State Historic Parks, Michigan, for his photographic work.

I thank also Carl R. Nold and David A. Armour, Director and Deputy Director respectively of the Mackinac State Historic Parks, for their steady support of this project, and the editorial staff of the Michigan State University Press for their helpful contributions.

While I am indebted to all those mentioned here for their assistance, the responsibility for the contents of this book remains mine alone.

Joseph L. Peyser

I. INTRODUCTION

CHARLES DE RAYMOND

In 1754 the French and English in North America stood at the brink of a major conflict, the French and Indian War, that would forever alter the cultural and political landscape of the continent. Charles de Raymond, a captain in the *Troupes de la Marine*, the French colonial regular troops, had served in New France for 32 years. Frustrated in his efforts to win promotion or a choice frontier post where he could engage in the profitable fur trade, Raymond wrote a critical account of the state of affairs in New France just as France and England were about to escalate their recent armed clashes in North America to full-scale warfare. In this account, which he called his *dénombrement de tous les postes du Canada* (*Enumeration of all the Canadian posts*), Raymond chronicled bureaucratic inefficiency and corruption, discussed diplomatic relations between the French and the Indians, analyzed military and trade strategies, and put forth his own solutions to the problems he identified. In short, he provides his readers with a comprehensive, although strongly biased, overview of New France as it entered its final years as a colony of France. A complete translation of Raymond's *Enumeration of all the Canadian posts* begins on page 49.

Raymond arrived in Canada as a second ensign in 1722 and was promoted to full ensign in 1731. In 1738 he was promoted to lieutenant and to the command of Fort Niagara, a command he held until 1746. In that year he was promoted to captain and fought against the English in New York and Massachusetts during King George's War (1744-48, the North American phase of the War of the Austrian Succession, 1740-48). In 1748 Commandant General Roland-Michel Barrin de La Galissonière reassigned Raymond to the Niagara command, but in 1749, before the arrival

1

The Cross of Saint Louis (*La Croix de Saint-Louis*) was awarded to Charles de Raymond upon his being received in 1754 as a *chevalier* in the Royal and Military Order of Saint Louis. This, the highest royal distinction to which a Canadian officer could aspire, was awarded by the king but rarely to officers of the *Troupes de la Marine* in New France. *Courtesy of Mackinac State Historic Parks, Michigan.*

in Quebec of the new governor general, Jacques-Pierre de Taffanel de La Jonquière, La Galissonière appointed this seasoned officer to command the Miami post (now Fort Wayne, Indiana). Although this post was located among the turbulent Miamis, Raymond nonetheless rejoiced over finally being granted a post with trading rights. La Jonquière, however, dissatisfied with Raymond's failure to win back the defecting Miamis, recalled him from the post in 1750, after only one year. After a short assignment in Louisbourg in 1752-53, the disgruntled Raymond briefly returned to France in 1754, where he was admitted as a *chevalier* (knight) by Louis XV to the Royal and Military Order of Saint-Louis.[1]

As the spring of 1754 approached, the new *chevalier* saw his prospects in New France brightening. On 18 April the minister of Marine (colonial affairs) wrote the new governor general, Ange de Menneville Duquesne, the following letter in support of Raymond:

To M. le Marquis Duquesne

Versailles 18 April 1754

Sieur de Raymond, a captain in the Canadian troops who came to France in charge of the dispatches from Ile Royale [Cape Breton Island] gave me a description of his services. He has in fact performed some that deserve attention, and at all times salutary reports have come back about his zeal and diligence. It is up to you to propose the rewards that he deserves, according to the opportunities that occur for his promotion. But while waiting you should be able to find an opportunity to assign him to some special command that can be of some advantage to him. I am asking you to do it as long as that can be reconciled with the arrangements you have to make for the good of the service. The experience that he has acquired in these kinds of missions has put him in a position to be successfully employed in them. And I shall be most pleased furthermore for you to be able to do something for him, in respect to several esteemed individuals under whose protection he is and who have recommended him to me very highly.

I am entirely, Sir, your obedient etc.[2]

Upon Raymond's return to Quebec in the fall of 1754, Duquesne brusquely turned him down for a promotion or another lucrative assignment despite the minister's high recommendation. The reasons Duquesne gave for rejecting advancement for Raymond are contained in the governor's stinging appraisal of Raymond's ideas, motives, and performance that he sent to the minister:

Quebec, 7 October 1754

My Lord,

Your recommendation for Sieur de Raymond, a captain in this colony, would be an order for me if there were an opportunity for promotion or some vacant post that could be appropriate for him, and it is distressing for me not to be in a position to provide him with this last advantage because it would not be fair to displace prematurely an officer who is performing well.

I did not meet M. de Raymond, who still remained at Ile Royale at the time of my arrival in Canada. This officer showed me the statement of his service that he padded and greatly embellished. I found his report very excessive and his pretensions as mad as they are strange, since he wants to establish high, middle, and low levels of justice among the northern Indians.[3] I am willing to believe that if he had been less disinterested, he would have earned beyond ten thousand écus[4] which the Miami post brought him, but what reassures me on his account because of the interest that you are taking in him, My Lord, is the fact that he is living in easy circumstances and that he is very carefully saving his money while waiting for the opportunity to be placed suitably to increase his fortune, with which he appears to me to be very preoccupied.

I am with deep respect, My Lord, your most humble and obedient servant.

Duquesne[5]

The contents of Duquesne's letter raise some questions. It is possible but unlikely that Raymond profited to the extent of 30,000 livres during the one year he spent at the Miami post. The defection of the Miami chief La Demoiselle and his followers, the competition and disruption coming from George Croghan and other English traders at Pickawillany and elsewhere, and the turmoil in the upper country (the Great Lakes Basin)

The Duquesne family coat of arms with silver shield and rampant black lion trimmed in red with a red tongue, registered in 1700 in the name of Abraham Duquesne and his wife, Ursule Posselle, the governor general's parents. The governor's coat of arms added the cordon of the Royal and Military Order of Saint Louis around the shield. It was surmounted by a marquis's coronet, later topped by an Indian's arm and tomahawk symbolizing his wartime service as governor general of New France. *From the fonds Maurice Brodeur (P574), Archives nationales du Québec, Centre de Québec. Courtesy of National Archives of Canada.*

could only have had a detrimental effect on the post's trade. Duquesne had arrived in New France in 1752, several years after Raymond had left the Miamis, and he may well have been reporting hearsay about Raymond's supposed profit.

On the other hand, Montreal notarial records show that in June 1751 Raymond provided on credit 9,435 livres in trade goods and money to Pierre Leduc (Le Duc) *dit* Souligny, a merchant-voyageur, to supply Souligny's upper country trading trip. In June 1752 Raymond provided on credit an additional 7,394 livres of trade goods to Souligny for another such trip. Since Raymond had not been permitted to trade at Niagara, the king's post that he commanded for so long, it may well be that the nearly 17,000 livres that he invested in Souligny's ventures came from his one year at the Miami post, thereby lending some credibility to Duquesne's comment.[6]

As for Raymond's reported suggestion of establishing three levels for administering justice to the Indians, I have to date found no mention of this concept elsewhere in Raymond's correspondence. Considering his long experience as an upper country commander among the Indians, it remains to be seen just how "strange" his ideas may have been. As for his "padding" the statement of his service, it was common practice for officers to embellish their service in seeking promotion; Raymond was not unusual in this regard. Duquesne clearly had other reasons for the manner in which he turned Raymond down.[7]

Soon after his cold reception by Duquesne, the frustrated Raymond sent his bold *Enumeration of all the Canadian posts* to a highly placed and influential friend in France, Colonel Michel Le Courtois de Surlaville. The man to whom the 48-year-old captain sent his exposé was about eight years younger than Raymond and had been a colonel since 1751. Surlaville, a rising star in the French army, had been wounded twice in Europe during the War of the Austrian Succession, and his valor at Fontenoy in 1745 had won him the Cross of Saint-Louis. In 1751 the newly named governor of Ile Royale, Count Jean-Louis de Raymond (Charles de Raymond's cousin), had requested that Surlaville accompany him in the capacity of troop major of Louisbourg.[8] Charles de Raymond was one of two Canadian officers sent there with their companies by Governor General La Jonquière to serve under Surlaville and Jean-Louis de Raymond. At the end of one year, in 1753, Charles returned to France on the same ship as his cousin and his new friend, Surlaville. After Charles's return to Quebec in late 1754, he and Surlaville continued to

Notarial deed of Pierre Leduc *dit* Souligny's obligation for 9,435 livres of trade goods received on credit from Charles de Raymond, 21 June 1751. *Archives nationales du Québec, Direction de l'Ouest du Québec, Notaire J.-B. Adhémar, CN 601, S3 P11058.*

correspond with each other, and this correspondence included the *Enumeration of all the Canadian posts*.[9]

DESCRIPTION OF RAYMOND'S *ENUMERATION* OF *ALL THE CANADIAN POSTS*

Raymond's *Enumeration of all the Canadian posts*, sent to Surlaville in 1754, a crucial moment in North American colonial history, provides a remarkably candid and detailed report on and recommendations for New France on the eve of the Seven Years' War. From the report it is evident that Raymond hoped Surlaville would present it to the new minister of Marine, Jean-Baptiste Machault d'Arnouville, in hopes of advancing Raymond's career.

Raymond's treatise, for despite the fact that he called it an enumeration it is much more than that, deals extensively with the French posts in the *pays d'en haut* (upper country). His sweeping analysis, however, extends from the post at Michilimackinac on the strait between Lakes Michigan and Huron to as far east as the commerce, ports, and defenses of Acadia on the Atlantic coast. Raymond's stated purpose in writing to his friend, whom he addressed in his first sentence as "My dear Surlaville," was "to satisfy" him by providing him with a frank, detailed "enumeration" or, more accurately, assessment of the current system of administration of the French posts. He included the posts throughout the Great Lakes Basin, what is now upper New York State, the Ohio River Valley, and the disputed colony of Acadia.

Raymond's report does not simply consist of lists; it goes far beyond a mere enumeration of posts. It is actually a critique of the then-current organization and administration of the posts, supported by specific figures on costs and by his own detailed observations on abuses of the system. He makes recommendations for the reform of the system, then riddled with favoritism and corrupt officers and civil authorities; offers strategic observations regarding the English colonies and their implications for the French posts; proposes a river-and-lake transportation system; reports on the underpayment of officers and its disastrous consequences; and moves beyond military and administrative concerns to discuss social issues as well, commenting on colonial French men and women and their mores. Raymond provides observations on Indian customs and suggestions for improving relations between the French and their Native American allies, and makes recommendations on the inconsistent practices of both church and government regarding the brandy trade. He criticizes certain missionaries and missions and makes specific suggestions for reducing large-scale smuggling and fraud.

Raymond's reforms for the officer corps and the military include assigning only worthy senior officers (captains) to command the posts; discontinuing the practice of appointing junior officers as commandants through favoritism; discontinuing the award of certain posts' trade to the commandants, replacing that practice with standardized levels of supplementary pay for all post commanders and subordinate officers; and increasing the strength of certain garrisons and decreasing that of others.

Raymond's recommendations for trade and finance involve putting all the posts on the *congé* (trade license) system, with the price of congés (purchased by merchants) restored from 600 to 1,000 livres; having the king pay all officers and employees at the posts from the proceeds of the sale of congés, rather than having the commandant-proprietors pay them; establishing certain new posts and closing others; opening the brandy trade to all, both officers and merchants; shifting to the merchants the costs of transporting goods and supplies to all the posts; and instituting measures to eliminate fraudulent practices at the posts. His suggestions for the colony's trade include merging the Acadian fur trade with that of Canada, and leasing out Acadian seal-hunting rights rather than awarding them free to private parties. Raymond estimates the king's annual savings from his proposed reforms to be over 183,000 livres.

Raymond's central theme is that instituting his reforms will produce vast savings for the king, but throughout the report a hidden agenda becomes increasingly clear. This does not become obvious until more than 50 pages into the report, when he sets forth various proposals for his own elevation in rank and for assignment to command one of the most lucrative posts.[10] Nevertheless his case for reform was sufficiently persuasive for Surlaville to submit over his own name a modified version of the report to the minister. Raymond's treatise, as indicated above, provides a profusion of details on many aspects of French commercial and military life on the frontier in addition to French and Indian interchanges. It could only have been written by an officer with his experience and service in many parts of the French frontier.

Raymond's report is unique in its time frame for the comprehensiveness of its coverage, its authoritativeness, and the writer's forthrightness and boldness in presenting his observations and criticisms of the system. In my judgment, the only other French post commander to produce lengthy written reports of comparable characteristics was the prolific Antoine Laumet *dit* de Lamothe Cadillac over a half century earlier. While Cadillac's written expression is more eloquent and polished than Raymond's, both men's styles are rich in metaphors and color. Just as Cadillac's early letters provide an overview of the upper country and the colony near the start of the eighteenth century, Raymond's highly detailed exposé is a source of new information on conditions in the posts and society of New France on the eve of its conquest.

Raymond's knowledge of New France beyond the limits of the lower (main) colony along the Saint Lawrence River is extensive in scope. He conceptualizes the far-flung parts of the French North American empire in 1754 as a potentially unified whole, both strategically and commercially. His recommendations are supported by specifics—for each post and globally—such as salaries; weights and quantities of supplies; prices; monthly rations for civilians and soldiers; types of equipment used in water and land transportation; supplies needed for repairs; numbers of men needed for garrisons or for transportation; numbers of trade licenses; numbers of chimney sweeps for the posts and their wages; numbers of wagoners, blacksmiths, cowherds, bakers, millers, and interpreters needed at individual posts and their wages; types and amounts of food and drink and their cost for each post's officers, commanders' and storekeepers' wives, chaplains, surgeons, and the sick; and gifts needed for Indians.

The ensuing report, based on Raymond's *dénombrement*, was officially presented to the minister by Surlaville after substantial editing. Surlaville's official *Mémoire en forme d'observations concernant le dénombrement des postes de Canada* is shorter than Raymond's original by one-third. The changes include, among others, deletion of Raymond's identifications of those officers—mostly well-known upper country commandants—and civilians intent upon enriching themselves rather than serving the king, and removal of his recommendations regarding the brandy trade. The report was reorganized into a drier, less sensational, and more sequential presentation. Raymond's frequently quaint spelling and grammar were largely corrected, and many of his sentences were rephrased. The version laid by Surlaville before the minister, while substantially the same as Raymond's, conveyed a somewhat different view of the colony to the minister, but in it Surlaville retained all of Raymond's key recommendations (other than the one on the brandy trade).[11]

The "originals" of these two unsigned and undated *mémoires* were found in 1923 in the archives of the Séminaire de Saint-Sulpice in Paris by the distinguished Montreal historian Aegidius Fauteux. His description of the two documents and his dating of them are contained in his article "Le Chevalier de Raymond" which precedes his transcript of the Raymond *dénombrement* in the 1927-28 *Rapport de l'archiviste de la province de Québec* (*RAPQ*) on pages 317-22 and 323-54, respectively. (This article is translated and annotated in appendix 2 of the present work.) In the Sulpician archives, the copy of the *dénombrement* is bound into a register titled *Pièces pour l'histoire militaire du Canada, 1730-1760*. The register is classified as *Manuscrit 1200*, and the *dénombrement* is designated as *Pièce n° 35*, on folios 135 recto to 170 verso. The copy of Surlaville's *mémoire* that Fauteux reported is *Pièce n° 38* on folios 181 recto to 215 verso. (*Pièce n° 40* on folios 218 recto to 235 verso in the same volume, not reported by Fauteux, is another copy—not in Surlaville's handwriting—of Surlaville's *mémoire*, apparently identical in content to *Pièce n° 38*.)

Neither *Pièce n° 35* nor *Pièce n° 38* appears to be an original, both almost certainly being copies by different eighteenth-century scribes. The copy of Raymond's original shows obvious great care in reproducing faithfully Raymond's own phraseology and spelling.[12] Fauteux's transcript, published in *RAPQ*, differs from the copy in the seminary archives in that he created paragraphs where Raymond did not, corrected spelling errors, modernized imperfect and conditional verb endings, corrected grammatical errors, and occasionally changed Raymond's wording.

Another transcript of the Raymond document, along with one of the Surlaville report, was made between 1926 and 1928 by an unknown individual for the Public Archives of Canada (now the National Archives of Canada, abbreviated in the present work as NAC).[13] These very accurate handwritten transcripts faithfully reproduce the Paris documents, and are available to the public. The Raymond *dénombrement* transcript is catalogued in the NAC Manuscript Division as manuscript MG 17, A 7-1, volume 4, pages 2895 through 2983. The Surlaville *mémoire* is in the same volume, on pages 2998 through 3055. Photocopies of these two documents are available from the National Archives of Canada.

In order to establish the definitive eighteenth-century documents rather than base my translation on twentieth-century transcripts, I went to the Séminaire de Saint-Sulpice in Paris in October 1994. There I collated the NAC transcripts of both the Raymond and Surlaville documents with the original scribes' copies. In addition I obtained the kind permission of the seminary's archivist to have the originals and *Pièce n° 40*, the handwritten draft of the Surlaville *mémoire*, microfilmed in Paris. The microfilm of these three documents is now housed in the research library of Mackinac State Historic Parks in Lansing, Michigan.

HISTORICAL BACKGROUND TO 1754

In 1713 the Treaty of Utrecht ended both the War of the Spanish Succession in Europe (1702-13) and its North American phase, Queen Anne's War, which had pitted France and England against each other. The treaty, which ushered in a 30-year period of peace between the two colonial rivals, required France to give up a substantial number of its European and North American territories. From New France, commonly called Canada by both the French and the English, Great Britain acquired "for ever . . . the Bay and Streights of Hudson, . . . all *Nova Scotia* or *Accadie*, with its ancient Boundaries, as also the City of Port Royal, now called Annapolis Royal, . . . [and] The Island called *Newfoundland*, with the adjacent Islands." France, however, was allowed "to catch Fish, and to Dry them" on the north shore of Newfoundland, a concession of major importance to the French. Article XV of the treaty recognized the five Iroquois nations as subjects of Great Britain and further provided that the Indian allies of both European powers "shall enjoy full liberty of going and coming on account of Trade" from one colony to the other.[14]

The terms of the treaty signed by Louis XIV seemed to signal the forthcoming economic collapse of New France and ascendancy of the British in North America. New France's North Atlantic territories—with the exception of desolate Cape Breton Island and the islands of Saint-Pierre and Miquelon, which remained French—were gone. The French share of the rich northwest fur trade at Hudson Bay was eliminated; the powerful Iroquois, trading partners and military allies of the English, now had the right to send emissaries to Canada to entice freely the French-allied tribes with inexpensive and high-quality trade goods and cheap rum; and the French-allied tribes were allowed to go to English posts to trade. The French felt the English closing in on them from Hudson Bay, from Acadia,[15] from Carolina (into Louisiana[16]), and from New England as the English colonies spread their trade networks into the continent's interior. France had to find a way to save its colony from being reduced to insignificance.

The first step in New France's recovery was the establishment by the French of a settlement, port, and fortress at Louisbourg on Cape Breton Island, which the French renamed Ile Royale. This strategic stronghold

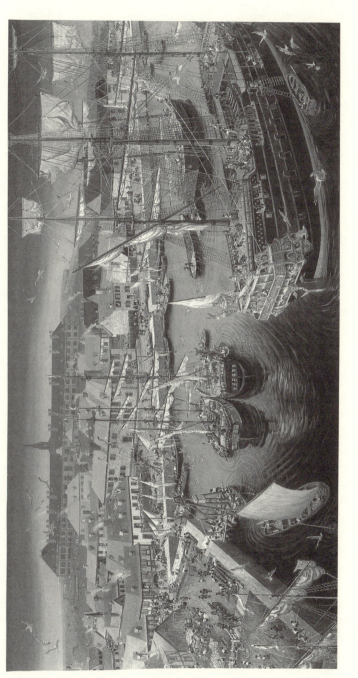

View from a warship of the quayside of Fortress Louisbourg, 1744. *Reproduced with permission of the artist, Lewis Parker; photograph courtesy of Parks Canada, Fortress of Louisbourg National Historic Site.*

preserved France's presence on the Atlantic seaboard, providing a number of major advantages: its port and supplies were of great value to French shipping engaged in trade between France, its Caribbean islands, and Canada; it protected and provisioned the fishing fleet; by means of a fleet based there, it could guard the mouth of the St. Lawrence River and its access to Quebec and the interior; and, in time of war, it could serve as a staging area for attacking the English colonies' coastal settlements and for-tifications as well as attack their shipping.[17]

In the years following the Treaty of Utrecht, in order to retain its Indian allies and prevent the English from expanding into the interior, France reestablished and strengthened its chain of strategically located for-tified posts. These posts bracketed all five of the Great Lakes, secured the Mississippi and other rivers, and strengthened the Louisiana colony. In the 1730s, the French established ten or more posts to the northwest of Lake Superior (a region they called "The Western Sea") and competed effec-tively with Hudson Bay for the high-quality fur trade in the north.[18]

In addition to strengthening their forts and trading posts, the French continued to send missionaries to the allied tribes of the *pays d'en haut*. The reasons for continuing state support of the missions were concisely expressed in the minutes of a 1718 meeting of the Council of Marine in Paris, in which Governor General Philippe de Rigaud de Vaudreuil's request for additional missionaries was approved:

> Of all the means that can be used to keep the Indians on our side, there is none more effective than giving them missionaries, because these missionaries by teaching them the principles of religion hold them by the influence they acquire over their minds and render them more peaceful. . . . The Jesuit fathers are the most capable of leading the Indians. It is certain that they serve both religion and the state equally well, and it is desirable that six come from France next year.[19]

Many of the posts in the *pays d'en haut* were composed of small gar-risons of *Troupes de la Marine* (regular colonial troops); a trading post for Indians and traders, with a warehouse for the bales of furs to be shipped to Montreal; and a mission. These three elements of the French culture were dependent upon each other for success in the wilderness. The key element in France retaining its hegemony in its vast sphere of influence was con-tinued support from the posts' Indian hosts and clients. This support included hundreds of allied Indian warriors assembled at each post in times of need to fight against the English or Indian enemies of the French.[20]

During this postwar recovery period the English were far from idle. In response to the construction of a French trading post on the Niagara River in 1720, the English built a trading post in 1724 at Oswego on the southeast shore of Lake Ontario. This post became a tremendous problem for the French by virtue of its inexpensive trade goods and liquor, which the French-allied Indians—and even a number of French traders—could not resist. By 1727 the French had completed the stone Fort Niagara, and the same year the English began construction of a stone fort at Oswego. The loss of trade at the French posts enraged the French to such an extent that in 1727 Governor General Charles de La Boische de Beauharnois issued orders to "send a detachment of soldiers and militiamen without delay to prevent the construction of the Oswego house [i.e., stone fort] and to chase the English from that post." Beauharnois quickly rescinded his "hasty action," however, in view of the likely consequences from the Iroquois, and Louis XV's prior instructions to avoid direct confrontation. The destruction of the fort at Oswego remained a high priority for New France, but the state of peace between England and France prevented any military action for the time being.[21]

The three decades of peace between France and England did not mean that all was quiet throughout New France. The French persisted in their efforts to expand the fur trade to the northwest of the Mississippi among the Sioux and other western tribes. In so doing, they bypassed the Foxes (or Mesquakies) of Wisconsin, thereby setting the stage for the sporadic Fox Wars, which cost the French heavily from 1712 to 1735. While the Canadian French and their allies were struggling with the Foxes, the Louisiana French, aided by their allies the Choctaws, were fighting for their lives, first against the Natchez in 1729, then against the Chickasaws in the 1730s and 1740.[22]

In both the Fox and the Chickasaw Wars the French suffered shocking defeats before overcoming their adversaries. The Chickasaws came to terms with the French only with the bold intervention of strong contingents of French *Troupes de la Marine* and allied Indians from the upper country posts and Montreal, including French-allied Christian Iroquois from the Montreal area missions. Both the Foxes and the Chickasaws were finally neutralized by 1742, but relations between England and France had worsened in Europe to the point of hostilities in 1743 and a declaration of war in 1744.[23]

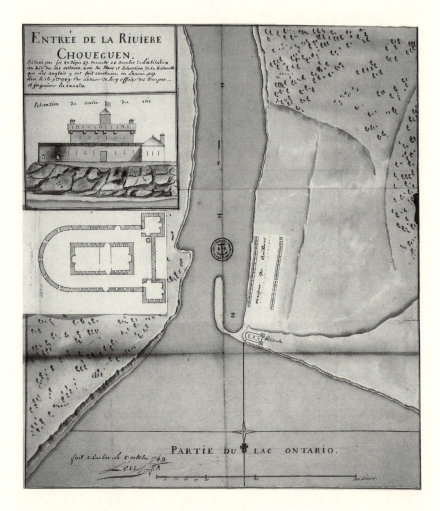

Plan of Fort Oswego and adjacent fur traders' houses at the mouth of the
Oswego River, drawn in 1749 by Chaussegros de Léry *fils*. North is to the
bottom of this plan. *"Entrée de la rivière Chouegen et du fort que les anglais y ont
fait construire, par Chaussegros de Léry fils, ingénieur," aquarelle sur papier, 8 octobre
1749.* D.F.C. *Amérique septentrionale 1I/5PFB/533, Centre des Archives d'Outre-
mer, Aix-en-Provence (Archives nationales, France). Reproduced by permission.*

The North American extension of the War of the Austrian Succession, King George's War, pitted the French and their Indian allies against the English colonies with their Mohawk allies from 1744 to 1748. The main action during the early years of the war occurred in Acadia, with the French launching an unsuccessful assault from Louisbourg against Annapolis Royal in 1744. In retaliation, the New Englanders sent a large force under William Pepperrell, supported by a British naval squadron, to attack Louisbourg. On 17 June 1745, after a seven-week siege, the fortress guarding the main supply route to New France surrendered. For the duration of the war, the English succeeded in choking off the flow of goods into Canada from France.[24]

The fighting continued in 1746 and 1747 with large-scale French and Indian raids into British Acadia and New England and a massive but disastrously unsuccessful French naval expedition to retake Louisbourg and Acadia. By 1747, the fall of Louisbourg had resulted in another front opening against the French in the *pays d'en haut*. The lack of trade goods and skyrocketing prices of scarce French commodities alienated a number of the French-allied tribes. They were further incited by English traders, mostly from Pennsylvania, who had moved into the Ohio Valley and along the southern shore of Lake Erie. English traders like George Croghan traded at Sandusky, Pickawillany (Piqua, Ohio), and Cuyahoga (near today's Cleveland). They drew a number of the French allies to them and aggressively won their support to thrust further into the sphere of French influence to the west. In 1747 bands from several of the western tribes, including the Hurons, Ottawas, Chippewas, and Miamis, rose up against the French in the so-called Huron Conspiracy, attacking and looting French trading posts, killing parties of French traders, and seriously threatening Detroit and Michilimackinac.[25]

In response the French sent strong reinforcements to both Detroit and Michilimackinac while other post commanders adroitly dealt with the disaffected Indian nations by threatening to prevent the French traders from going to them. Further, several tribal chiefs visiting in Quebec observed the arrival of three French ships, including a storeship bringing needed trade goods, that had run the English blockade. Upon returning to the *pays d'en haut*, the chiefs conveyed what they had seen to their tribes. These factors enabled the French to weather the storm in the west which, near the end of their war with the English, had constituted a major threat to New France.[26]

The Treaty of Aix-la-Chapelle in 1748 ended the war, restored Louisbourg to the French, and enabled them to lower the prices of their trade goods. Most of the tribes were placated, but a pro-English faction of Miamis remained disaffected and was increasingly attracted to the English. In 1743 the English had ventured well west of the Appalachians to establish the busy trading post of Pickawillany on the Great Miami River less than 100 miles southeast of the long-established French Fort Miami (Fort Wayne, Indiana). This was the westernmost penetration of the English into Indian territory within the French sphere of influence north of the Ohio River and its success was an immediate threat to the French.

In June of 1749, in response to the encroaching English traders and agents of the Ohio Company (composed of land speculators from Virginia) who were preparing to settle the Ohio Valley, Commandant-General of New France Roland-Michel Barrin de La Galissonière sent Captain Pierre-Joseph Céloron de Blainville with a detachment of over 200 men to reestablish the French claim to the entire region. Part of this mission was to map the area, and the foresighted La Galissonière assigned the task to the Jesuit priest and hydrographer Joseph-Pierre Bonnécamps. Céloron's other mission was to win back the defecting Indians. In September, nearly at the end of his mission, Céloron reached Pickawillany, where the village of the pro-English Miami chief La Demoiselle (also known as Memeskia and Old Britain) was located. The reception there was so hostile that Céloron lost no time in moving on to Fort Miami and then back to Montreal where he gave his report to the new governor general, Jacques-Pierre de Taffanel de La Jonquière. The presence and influence of the English throughout the entire disputed region from the Allegheny River to Pickawillany were cause for alarm.[27]

Several weeks before Céloron arrived at Fort Miami, the commandant of that post, Captain Charles de Raymond (whose 1754 treatise is the subject of this book), had written two letters to La Jonquière describing the tense state of affairs in the Miami country and the Ohio Valley to the east. The visible anxiety expressed by Raymond in these two letters undoubtedly stemmed in part from his knowledge that only two years earlier, a French trading post in the Miami country had been attacked by Miamis, who killed five *engagés* (fur-trade employees) at the post, carried away the proprietor's furs and trade goods, and burned the building.[28] The translations of these letters, dated 4 September and 5 September 1749, follow:[29]

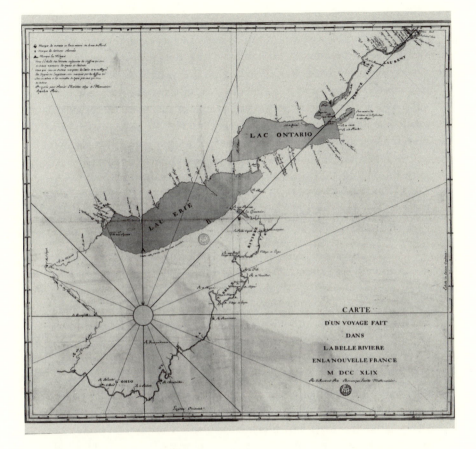

Bonnécamps' map of Céloron's 1749 expedition through the Ohio River Valley from Lake Erie to the Great Miami River. To strengthen France's claim to the disputed territory, Céloron buried a half-dozen engraved lead plates from the Allegheny River to the mouth of the Great Miami River (*Rivière à la Roche*), whose locations Bonnécamps marked on this map. La Demoiselle's village and his portage trail from the Great Miami River to Fort Miami are also shown. *Carte d'un voyage fait dans la Belle Rivière en la Nouvelle France, 1749, par le Révérend Père Bonnécamps, reproduced by permission of the Service historique de la Marine, Recueil 67, n° 21; photograph courtesy of the National Archives of Canada, Ph/903/1749.*

At the Miami post 4 September 1749

Sir:

It has been represented to you that the band of Miamis that withdrew to the Great Miami River [*la rivière à la Roche*, i.e., Pickawillany] were asking to come back to this post. It appears to be a very long way from that. The English are sparing nothing in order to keep them there and to entice the rest of those who are here. The excessive price of the French merchandise in this post, the great bargains that the English are giving them and the big presents that they are giving to the nations have entirely disposed them in their favor and induce them to withdraw to their place. We have made peace with the English, yet in this region they do not stop working toward making war on us through the Indians and inciting them to a general revolt against the French as part of their plan to succeed in making themselves masters of all the *pays d'en haut.*

It is useless to delude ourselves that the Indians are well disposed toward us. There is only the most misleading of appearances. They are more ill-intentioned than ever. A hidden rumor is spreading that all the nations of this region are working on a general conspiracy against the French in the posts of the *pays d'en haut.* Nothing is more certain than the fact that the English have had forty horses loaded with powder, a great quantity of sabers and musketballs brought in and distributed in 70 or 80 villages in all directions from the Ohio River. 300 Englishmen are spreading into all the villages. They have built three forts in different locations, in which there are officers, swivel guns [*perriers*], and grenade mortars. They gave Nicolas two swivel guns and two of their grenade mortars.[30] They told all the nations, having found out about M. de Céloron's expedition: The Frenchman is marching upon you to chase you away from here. We shall defend you, but if the Frenchman wants to fight, we shall fight with you against him. The Shawnees replied: The Frenchmen are marching with but a handful of people. They are coming only to ask forgiveness from the nations that have struck them.

The nations are however uneasy on seeing the French marching, which arouses great suspicions that can only produce a very bad result. I shall do my best to have the bad Miami come back. Le Pied Froid [Coldfoot], who is the great chief of this whole nation,[31] told me that he did not think they could be made to break off from the English who were giving them all their merchandise at low prices. M. Dubuisson[32] assures me that he is an honest man who can be counted upon. I believe it if it is true that there might be honest people among the Indians.

I have the honor of being with the deepest respect, Sir, your most humble and obedient servant.

de Raymond

The morning after Raymond dispatched his letter to the governor general, he received a visit from Pied Froid which prompted the following to La Jonquière:

At the Miami post 5 September 1749

Sir:

Since my written letters, Pied Froid, the great chief of the Miami, the war chief, and the elders came this morning. They provided me in great detail with the news that is being poured forth everywhere. There can be some truth and some falsehood in it, and here in general is the summary of what it contains.

That there are war flags, wampum belts, peace pipes, strings of red wampum, and red and black blankets which are being run to all the nations of the *pays d'en haut* to hatch a general conspiracy to destroy all the French who are there, in order to have on their land only their brother, the Englishman; that the autumn will not go by without some Frenchmen being killed; that I was to be attacked in the Miami post; that the betrayal was an accomplished fact; that they had been the first to be informed; that we had not been willing to believe them; that all the Detroit nations were part of this treason and that under the pretext of going to winter quarters, they were to go to the Ohio River to carry out the plan; that M. de Céloron had been held up to ridicule; that they had axed his flag and that he would not leave the Ohio River without Frenchmen being killed.

This speech was followed by three wool blankets and by four strings of wampum that the war chief received last night on behalf of La Demoiselle's band which was asking him for help, which he showed me; and he gave me the 4 enclosed strings of wampum accompanied by big, beautiful promises of loyalty on which I am not counting, and [he told me] that their heart was French and they would die with the French; and he assured me and all the chiefs that they sent word to La Demoiselle and his band that they were rejecting his speech that they would not listen to; that they would not be involved in his treason and the proof that he was giving him was that he had turned over to his father the four strings of wampum and that they were all devoted to the French.

The above-mentioned enclosed four strings of wampum that I took [from Pied Froid] were being brought from the direction of the St. Joseph River [Fort St. Joseph, now Niles, Michigan]. Although Pied Froid and his band appear to have good intentions, I do not trust them and I shall follow the advice that he gave me, which is to protect myself and to fortify the fort, which is scarcely possible, unless we build a new one.

I have the honor [etc.]

de Raymond[33]

The tense situation in the Miami country and to the east in the Ohio River Valley continued unabated. English traders and their Iroquois emissaries continued to infiltrate the *pays d'en haut* to convince the French-allied tribes to revolt against the French. French attempts to mount an attack against La Demoiselle had not materialized. With the blessing and support of the English, the renegade Miami chief continued to participate in attempts to convince dissident Hurons, Miamis, Ouiatanons, Piankeshaws, Illinois, Ottawas, Shawnees, Delawares, and others to rise up against the French in the *pays d'en haut* and the Ohio Valley.[34] Raymond reported the extreme weakness of the Miami post in the face of the growing threat, as shown in the following two excerpts from letters he wrote to the governor general in May of 1750:

I am too weak to be able to parry and repulse the attack that our enemies are preparing for us. What can I do with 20 or so men that I have here and from whom 9 merchants and residents are withdrawing to Detroit shortly and who are sending all their cattle there in the next two days to avoid having their throats cut with them. . . .[35]

Drawing of Miami Chief Pacane, Pied Froid's nephew, ca. 1778. This drawing was done by Henry Hamilton, lieutenant governor of Detroit (1775-79),
who was accompanied by Pacane on the expedition against Vincennes in
1778. Houghton Library, Harvard University. *Reproduced with permission of the
Houghton Library.*

It was my feeling to have the interpreter leave in order for you to be informed by him personally about the general disorder among all the nations of this region whom we have absolutely no further reason to be able to count on and against whom substantial and prompt relief is needed. But fearing that after his departure something adverse to the safety of this post might occur and that it might be said that nothing would have happened if I had not had him leave, in order not to take anything upon myself, I had all the merchants assemble to know their opinion. They decided that he should remain and signed the present letter to affirm to you how badly strong reinforcements are needed to hold on to this post. . . . No one is keen on staying here and having his throat cut. I would not be able to speak to or understand the Indians without an interpreter, as I neither speak nor understand their language. . . .[36]

In July 1750, in an attempt to resolve the dangerous state of affairs in the *pays d'en haut*, La Jonquière recalled Charles de Sabrevois from his post as commandant of Detroit and Raymond from the Miami post. The governor replaced Sabrevois with Céloron, appointing him at the staff rank of major,[37] and replaced Raymond with Louis Coulon de Villiers, who, as a son of the commandant of Fort St. Joseph, had grown up alongside the resident Miamis and Potawatomis. Despite Raymond's objections, La Jonquière appointed Villiers because he was respected by the Miamis and, according to La Jonquière, he knew and was friendly with La Demoiselle and the other Miami chiefs. Villiers was instructed to bring La Demoiselle back into the fold and to build a new fort at his post.[38]

In 1751 La Jonquière ordered Céloron to attack and destroy the rebellious Miamis at Pickawillany. Céloron, who, like Raymond, had unsuccessfully attempted to persuade La Demoiselle to leave Pickawillany, declined to follow these orders, claiming he did not have enough Frenchmen and could not assemble enough reliable Indian allies. In the fall of that year two soldiers of the Fort Miami garrison were killed by La Demoiselle's warriors within one thousand feet of the fort. In view of Céloron's failure to attack La Demoiselle, a detachment of 272 French and Indians from Fort Michilimackinac under Charles-Michel Mouet de Langlade descended upon Pickawillany in June 1752, when most of the Miamis were away hunting. The allies besieged the fort and defeated the Miami defenders, in the process killing one of the eight English traders who were there, taking five traders prisoner (later taken to Montreal), and boiling and eating La Demoiselle. The late but sudden and decisive use of force on the part of the French and their allies convinced most of the Miamis to return to them, while a handful took refuge at Lower Shawnee Town at the mouth of the Scioto River (near Portsmouth, Ohio). With this action, it was clear that the French and English North American colonies were once again approaching a state of war.[39]

In 1752, Governor General Ange de Menneville Duquesne arrived in Quebec, replacing La Jonquière, who had died in office earlier that year. Duquesne found the colony in bad shape fiscally and strategically, and had received strict orders from Minister of Marine (colonial affairs) Antoine-Louis Rouillé to reduce expenditures for all the posts, and for the colony in general. Strategically, Duquesne, sensitive to the increasing English presence in the Ohio Valley and the lack of French forces there to enforce France's restated claim to the region, had to take action.

By 1753, the governor had ordered that the cost of all presents given to the posts' Indians must be borne by the merchant proprietors of the posts' trade. This procedure eliminated the system whereby the post commanders signed reimbursement certificates which were then presented by the merchants to the Marine Treasury in Quebec for payment. The minister correctly called the certificates "one of the most common and abusive excesses" among the colony's expenses, and wrote Duquesne that this was "the only way to avoid the abuse which was such a heavy burden to the king's treasury." In addition to abolishing the certificates, Duquesne eliminated the posts at Laprairie, the Lake of the Two Mountains, and the St. Louis Falls (Caughnawaka), all near Montreal. He also reduced expenditures at Detroit, Chambly, and Fort St. Jean, the last two on the Richelieu River east of Montreal.[40]

The minister had instructed Duquesne upon his appointment as governor to work with François Bigot, the intendant (top financial officer) of New France, to reduce the rapidly increasing expenses everywhere in the colony. This proved to be an elusive goal in view of Bigot's hidden large-scale corruption in league with many of the colony's officers. In the face of the English threat in the Ohio Valley, however, Duquesne was more successful; he took firm action to remove the English presence from the disputed territory, but the success came at tremendous cost.[41]

In the summer of 1753, despite marked opposition from the officers, Duquesne, following the court's instructions, sent a large force of two thousand troops and militiamen and several hundred allied Indians under Captain Paul Marin de La Malgue to occupy the Ohio Valley south of

Lake Erie as far as the Ohio River. Under incredibly difficult conditions, the detachment cleared a road from the south shore of Lake Erie—where they built Fort Presqu'Ile (Erie, Pennsylvania)—through the wilderness to the Rivière au Boeuf (Rivière aux boeufs; French Creek), a tributary of the Allegheny River.

At the Rivière au Boeuf the French erected a fort that they named *Fort de la rivière au Boeuf*, often referred to as Fort Le Boeuf (Waterford, Pennsylvania). They were able to proceed down the Rivière au Boeuf to its mouth at the Allegheny River, where they occupied Venango, the site of an old Indian town and an English trading post (later to be named Fort Machault after the new minister of Marine, Jean-Baptiste Machault d'Arnouville, appointed in 1754; now Franklin, Pennsylvania). Marin's exhausted men were too weakened, however, to complete their mission down the Allegheny another 80 miles to the forks of the Ohio where the Allegheny and Monongahela rivers join to form the Ohio. The French had suffered the loss of four hundred men to poor food, disease, and exhaustion, with hundreds of others too debilitated to proceed. The commander of the French forces, sick himself, died on 29 October 1753 at Fort Le Boeuf.[42]

Nevertheless this force had pushed most of the English traders out of the area and intimidated the Iroquois. Marin's replacement as commandant of the French forces in the Ohio Valley, Captain Jacques Legardeur de Saint-Pierre, arrived at Fort Le Boeuf on 3 December. On 12 December he received a young militia major named George Washington who presented Saint-Pierre with Virginia Governor Robert Dinwiddie's demand that the French depart from "the king of Great Britain's territories." Saint-Pierre carefully composed his response to Dinwiddie and gave it to Washington on the evening of 14 December. In the politest of terms, the French commander in chief wrote:

> As for the demand that you are making for me to withdraw, I do not believe that I am under any obligation to comply with it. Whatever your instructions might be, I am here in accordance with the orders of my general, and I pray you not to doubt for one instant that I am steadfastly determined to conform to them with all the exactitude and firmness that can be expected of the best officer. . . .[43]

Two months later, in February 1754, Duquesne sent eight hundred men under Captain Claude-Pierre Pécaudy de Contrecoeur to reinforce the

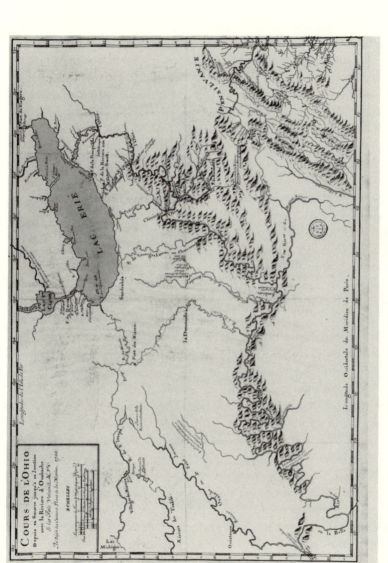
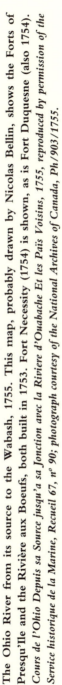

The Ohio River from its source to the Wabash, 1755. This map, probably drawn by Nicolas Bellin, shows the Forts of Presqu'Ile and the Rivière aux Boeufs, both built in 1753. Fort Necessity (1754) is shown, as is Fort Duquesne (also 1754). *Cours de l'Ohio Depuis sa Source jusqu'a sa Jonction avec la Rivière d'Ouabache Et les Païs Voisins, 1755, reproduced by permission of the Service historique de la Marine, Recueil 67, n° 90; photograph courtesy of the National Archives of Canada, Ph/903/1755.*

troops at Forts Presqu'Ile and Le Boeuf. Soon after Contrecoeur replaced the ailing Saint-Pierre as commandant, he moved down the Allegheny to the forks of the Ohio, where a unit of Virginia militiamen was beginning to erect a fort. Contrecoeur ordered the Virginians to leave, and he proceeded to construct Fort Duquesne (Pittsburgh, Pennsylvania) as his headquarters at that strategic location. The French now appeared to be well on the way to controlling the entire region west of the Alleghenies.[44]

Governor Dinwiddie meanwhile had sent a militia force of several hundred men under George Washington to reinforce the men at the forks of the Ohio. Contrecoeur reacted by sending a party of 33 men commanded by Ensign Joseph Coulon de Jumonville to hand Washington a summons to withdraw or be responsible for any subsequent hostilities. Washington led a group of about 40 militiamen and a number of Iroquois that proceeded to ambush the French party on 27 May, killing Jumonville and 9 men and capturing all but one of the rest, an act of murder according to the French. In response, Contrecoeur sent a detachment of 500 French soldiers and a contingent of allied Indians under the slain ensign's brother, Captain Louis Coulon de Villiers, to attack Washington's forces in the hastily constructed defenses that he called Fort Necessity (near Farmington, Pennsylvania).

After a short but bloody siege of the fort on 3 July 1754 (Washington's men suffered at least 100 casualties, including 30 dead; the French lost 3 dead and 17 wounded, including several Indians), Washington surrendered. Villiers permitted Washington and all but two of the other survivors to return to Virginia, and their fort and other buildings in the area were destroyed. Although France and England were technically at peace, the first shots of the French and Indian War, the North American phase of the Seven Years' War, had been fired. Both countries now began preparations on a grand scale for the coming conflict.[45]

On 31 May 1754, four days after Jumonville's patrol had been ambushed in Pennsylvania, the minister of Marine in Versailles had written to Duquesne concerning the great expenses being generated by its colony in North America. He wrote, "All resources are so depleted, that if things cannot be put back into the condition they were in before the advent of these immense fiscal excesses which we have been experiencing for some years, we shall be strongly compelled to abandon the colony. You will see what I am writing you jointly with M. Bigot [the intendant of New France] on that matter." The drain on the king's treasury was to increase, however, with Bigot and his officer cronies' accelerating corruption and

Fort Necessity (Farmington, Pennsylvania), on-site reconstruction of the 1754 fort. *Reproduced with permission of the National Park Service, Fort Necessity National Battlefield.*

rampant inflation compounded by the need to provision the French forces in the distant Ohio country.[46]

It was to a troubled colony that Raymond, with his new Cross of Saint Louis and his hopes high, returned in the fall of 1754. In Quebec his hopes were dashed by Duquesne, sorely pressed himself by highly placed critics for his costly campaign in the Ohio Valley and for his overall strategy. In the same set of dispatches to the minister containing his vicious 7 October 1754 rejection of Raymond's bid for advancement, Duquesne requested his own recall. It was at this time of crisis that the Chevalier de Raymond sent his revealing *dénombrement* to Colonel Surlaville, thereby making available to the minister a wealth of detail on the problems and ethos of New France.[47]

TOPICAL OUTLINE OF RAYMOND'S *ENUMERATION*

The structure of Raymond's report is outlined here, providing the reader with a table of contents. In Part IV of this book, an analysis is made of what Surlaville deleted, retained, and rephrased in his *mémoire*. In the analysis, several translated excerpts from Surlaville's report provide examples of the modifications in the document he presented to the minister. A topical outline of Surlaville's *mémoire* follows the comparative analysis, in appendix 1.

In the outline of Raymond's *dénombrement* presented here, the uppercase Roman numerals are Raymond's; the uppercase letters are mine. Boldface type is used for Raymond's bold heads and Roman numerals. The numbers in square brackets identify the National Archives of Canada transcript page numbers for reference purposes. The wording of the summarized content is mine.

Structure of Raymond's *Dénombrement*

I. Introduction stating the contents as the enumeration of all the Canadian posts; their locations; those that are king's posts; those that are trading posts; the present upkeep of the garrisons, the posts, and the commandants; the way to retain the Indian allies and prevent them from going to the English [NAC 2895]

A. **Northern posts** [NAC 2896-97]

B. **Southern posts** [NAC 2897-99]
Remarks on the choice of commandants, exposé of corruption and favoritism [NAC 2899-901]; remarks on the Indians' nature [NAC 2901-5]

C. **Detroit** [NAC 2905-7]
Criticism of governor generals, poor appointments of commandants and poor decisions in Acadia by the French command [NAC 2907-9]

D. Michilimackinac [NAC 2909-18]
Michilimackinac is on the Indians' route for trading at Oswego and Albany [NAC 2910-11]; Complaint about perceived injustices to himself and the other officers [NAC 2911-13]; plan to fortify three key passages, including Michilimackinac, to force Indians to stop trading with the English and to trade only with the French; importance of the Petit Rapide [NAC 2914-20]

II.   A. **The Petit Rapide**
The importance of the Petit Rapide in Raymond's proposed water transportation system for freight and trade

between Montreal and the upper country and Ohio River posts [NAC 2920-25]; Discussion of English encroachment on French territory from Oswego to Acadia [NAC 2925-28]

B. Long, detailed description—underlined—of favored officers and families and the posts granted them, inadequate pay to officers [NAC 2928-31]; short description—underlined—of Raymond's proposed system to correct inequities [NAC 2931-33]

C. Rationale for the commandants' supplementary pay and its funding through congés [NAC 2933-37]

D. The Merchants: Congés, water transportation of freight, competitive bidding for supplying the king's needs, quality control [NAC 2937-42]

E. **Determination** of garrison strength and employees for **La Présentation**, **Fort Frontenac**, **Niagara**, Le Petit Rapide [NAC 2942-45]; Recommendation to rectify the disparity in the posts' officers' pay by standardizing all the posts' salaries [NAC 2945-46]

F. **Regulation** of freightage allowances for commandants and officers; annual costs and savings for the king for the garrisons' rations, supplies, and boats [NAC 2946-49]

III.   A. **Garrison** strengths at the posts of the Belle Rivière, Detroit, Fort Duquesne, Rivière au Boeuf, Presqu'Ile, Miami, Ouiatanon; headquarters staffing at Detroit, Trois-Rivières, Michilimackinac [NAC 2949-51]

B. **Regulation and number** of congés for each post and income from the congés; recommendations for farming out the Acadian fur trade and sealing industry [NAC 2951-54]

C. Long digression—underlined—recommending opening the brandy trade to all, rather than granting it only to the favored few, who are named here [NAC 2954-58]

D. Supplementary pay recommended for the posts' officers, chaplains, surgeons, missionaries, and post employees, and amounts and cost of hay and firewood; tabulation [NAC 2962] showing an expected "profit" for the king of 40,425# after all expenses [NAC 2958-64]

E. Diatribe—underlined—on Abbé François Picquet and his post of La Présentation [NAC 2964-67]

F. Discussion of Indian customs, including gift-giving by the king to the Indians and the severe abuse by commandants of this practice [NAC 2967-70]; recommendations—underlined—for preventing the commandants' illegal trading of the king's presents [NAC 2970-72]

G. Present daily cost of rations and of supplementary pay for the garrisons that would be saved under the proposed plan [NAC 2972-79]

H. Short digression—underlined—on the irresponsibility and thievery that occur with the king's goods [NAC 2980-81]

I. Request for Surlaville's support of the proposal and for Raymond's elevation to inspector general, and plea for Surlaville's protection [NAC 2981-83]

NOTES

1. Pierre-Georges Roy, "Charles, Chevalier de Raymond," *Bulletin des recherches historiques* (hereafter cited as *BRH*), Lévis, Québec, 1948, 54:165-66; Aegidius Fauteux, "Le chevalier de Raymond," *Rapport de l'archiviste de la province de Québec* (hereafter cited as *RAPQ*) 1927-1928, 319-20. Fauteux's article (317-22) immediately precedes his transcript of the *dénombrement* (323-54) in the same issue, which he titled "Mémoire sur les postes du Canada adressé à M. de Surlaville, en 1754, par le Chevalier de Raymond." Appendix 2 of this work consists of an annotated translation of Fauteux's complete article on Raymond.

Although Fauteux (319) stated that Raymond was relieved from the Miami command in 1751, the latter's successor, Louis Coulon de Villiers, was sent by La Jonquière to command the Miami post in 1750, remaining in command there for three years (La Jonquière to Villiers, Montreal, 10 July 1750, Archives nationales, Colonies, Paris [hereafter cited as AN Col.], $C^{11}E$:194; Villiers to the minister, Montreal, 9 October 1754, AN Col., $C^{11}E$ 13:221-22).

Raymond fought alongside Jacques Legardeur de Saint-Pierre at the Battle of Lake George in 1755, in which Saint-Pierre died in action (see Joseph L. Peyser, *Jacques Legardeur de Saint-Pierre: Officer, Gentleman, Entrepreneur* [East Lansing and Mackinac Island: Michigan State University Press and Mackinac State Historic

Parks, 1996], 222-24). He distinguished himself in the Battle of Ticonderoga (Fort Carillon) in 1758, and was at the siege of Quebec in 1759. According to Fauteux's 1927-28 article (320), he was received as a *chevalier* in the Royal and Military Order of Saint-Louis in 1754; Pierre-Georges Roy set the date as 1753 (*BRH*, 54:166); Theodore Calvin Pease gave the date as 1759 (Theodore Calvin Pease and Ernestine Jenison, eds., *Collections of the Illinois State Historical Library*, [hereafter cited as *IHC*] 38 vols. [Springfield: Illinois State Historical Library, 1903-40], French Series vol. 3: *Illinois on the Eve of the Seven Years' War, 1747-1755*, 29:xxv). In 1940, Fauteux provided additional evidence, fixing the date as 18 January 1754 in *Les Chevaliers de Saint-Louis en Canada* (Montréal: Les Editions des Dix, 1940), 155. Raymond returned to France after the conquest, and died there in 1774.

2. Minister to Duquesne, Versailles, 18 April 1754, AN Col., B 99:180. Unless otherwise noted, all translations in this work are mine.

3. *Il veut établir une haute, moyenne et basse justice chez les sauvages du Nord.* These terms "have no exact equivalent in English" and are left in French in the English-language edition of volume 2 of the *Dictionary of Canadian Biography* (hereafter cited as *DCB*), 12 vols. (Toronto: University of Toronto Press, 1966-91), 2:xiii. *La haute, moyenne, et basse justice* were the three levels of French seignorial jurisdiction, adapted to New France, where the seigneur did not have the same rights as the feudal seigneurs in France.

   In his *The Seignorial System in Canada: A Study in French Colonial Policy* (New York: Longmans, Green, and Co., 1907), William Bennett Munro stated that "[T]he grant of the right of high jurisdiction (*haute justice*) gave the seignior [*sic*] power to deal with all criminal cases, including those punishable by death, mutilation, or other corporal penalty, with the exception only of such crimes as were deemed to be perpetrated directly against the royal person or property. . . . In civil cases the authority of the seignior possessing this degree of jurisdiction was without limit" (148). The seigneur with rights of middle jurisdiction (*moyenne justice*) had authority to adjudicate civil actions in which no more than the sum of 60 sols was in dispute (see note 4, following, for an explanation of the monetary units in New France), and criminal cases "in which the awardable penalty did not exceed the same sum" (150). The judicial authority of those seigneurs having the rights of low jurisdiction (*basse justice*) was limited to petty civil cases amounting to no more than 60 sols and criminal cases in which a penalty could not exceed 10 sols (150). Analyzing the seigneurs' infrequent use of their judicial power, Munro speculated that one of the reasons was that their decisions were all subject to appeal to the colony's royal courts (153).

   See also John A. Dickinson, "La Justice seigneuriale en Nouvelle-France: le cas de Notre-Dame-des-Anges," *Revue d'histoire de l'Amérique française* 28, no. 3 (décembre 1974): 323-46, and André Lachance, *La Justice criminelle du roi au Canada au XVIIIᵉ siècle: Tribunaux et officiers*, Les Cahiers d'histoire de l'Université Laval no. 22 (Québec: Les Presses de l'Université Laval, 1978), 11-12.

4. The official monetary unit in New France was the livre, worth 20 sols, each of which in turn was worth 12 deniers. An écu was worth 3 livres; a pistole was worth 10 livres. 10,000 écus (30,000 livres) was a substantial sum, equal in 1754 to almost 30 years of a captain's base pay, or 10 years of supplementary pay for commanding a post.

   The precise value of the livre in today's currency is virtually impossible to determine due to the many variables that affected it. On the basis of comparing prices in New France at different times with current U.S. prices, I would very roughly estimate the livre's value at 7 to 13 1995 U.S. dollars.

   The symbol for the livre was similar to our pound sign (#), but it had only one horizontal bar. In this book, # is used for the livre abbreviation, *s* for sols, and *d* for deniers. The amount of 10 livres, 17 sols, and 7 deniers would be abbreviated as 10# 17s 7d.

   See note 79 in Part III for the distinction between the monetary unit and the unit of weight which was also called the livre.

5. Duquesne to Minister, Quebec, 7 October 1754, AN Col., C^{11}A 99:257, translated by the present author. A transcript (with one minor error) and translation of this letter can be found in *IHC* 29:902-3.

6. Obligations de Pierre Leduc *dit* Souligny à Charles de Raymond, Montréal, le 21 juin 1751 et le 20 juin 1752, Archives nationales du Québec à Montréal (hereafter cited as ANQ-M), Greffe de J.-Bte Adhémar *dit* St.-Martin.

   If Raymond did succeed in enriching himself during his one year at the Miami post, his profits could have come from illegally trading brandy at his post, although there is no evidence that he engaged in this practice. Raymond signed a June 1750 voucher for 5,000# of merchandise delivered to him during the course of the year, "on the king's account and for the king's service," including 83 *pots* (half-gallons) of brandy at 20 livres per *pot*. He wrote that the prices he entered on the voucher were "according to the prices at which merchandise is sold at this post, particularly brandy which sells for twenty livres in furs per *pot*" (Etat des fournitures faites pour le compte et service du Roy par ordre de M. Raymond, fort des Miamis, 25 juin 1750, AN Col., C^{11}A, 119:145 recto-147 verso).

   The price of a *pot* of brandy at the Miami post in 1750 was 20 livres, whereas the intendant and governor approved the purchase of brandy in Montreal for the king's service that same year for 2 1/2 livres per *pot* (Etat de la Dépense que le Sr. Léchelle Négociant à Montréal a faite . . . , Montréal, le 16 juin 1750, AN Col., C^{11}A 96:327). Allowing for transport costs, the profit from brandy traded in the upper country was still very substantial. Just how much of a profit Raymond made at the Miami post is conjectural, as is the manner in which he made his profit.

   It is relevant to examine the financial experience of a Miami post commandant a few years before Raymond's assignment there. Jacques Legardeur de Saint-

Pierre, who commanded the Miami post from 1741 to 1744, purchased in June 1741 with his partner 24,000 *livres* of merchandise *on credit,* pledging all their possessions as security to the merchant who sold them the goods (just as Souligny pledged his possessions to Raymond).

By December 1742, Saint-Pierre was in arrears to his creditor for about 30,000 *livres,* counting heavily on a third-year profit to "protect me from owing for the rest of my days a sum that would be impossible for me ever to pay" (Obligation de Saint-Pierre et Clignancourt, associés, à Pierre Lestage, négociant, Montréal, le 15 juin 1741, ANQ-M, Greffe de Danré de Blanzy; Saint-Pierre à Beauharnois, le poste des Miamis, le 6 décembre 1742, Archives du Séminaire de Québec, Fonds Verreau, Carton 5, no. 7); for the translation and discussion of these and other pertinent documents, see Peyser, *Jacques Legardeur de Saint-Pierre,* chap. 2, passim.

Niagara was one of three king's posts, the other two being Detroit and Fort Frontenac, where the king retained the trading privilege in order to keep the cost of trade goods low enough to compete with the English post of Oswego (W. J. Eccles, *The Canadian Frontier, 1534-1760,* rev. ed. [Albuquerque: University of New Mexico Press, 1983], 146).

7. Duquesne was apparently unhappy as well with Louis Coulon de Villiers, Raymond's successor among the Miamis, failing to pay Villiers his supplementary pay as commandant for his last two years there and recalling him in 1753 (Villiers to the minister, Montreal, 9 October 1754, AN Col., $C^{11}E$ 13:221-22).

8. For an explanation of the staff rank of major in New France, see René Chartrand, *Canadian Military Heritage,* 3 vols. (Montreal: Art Global, 1993-), 1:107-8.

9. T. A. Crowley, "Le Courtois de Surlaville (Le Courtois de Blais de Surlaville), Michel," *DCB,* 4:443-44; Fauteux, "Le chevalier de Raymond," 319-20. Surlaville continued his illustrious military career during the Seven Years' War, first with an appointment in 1757 as assistant chief of the army staff under Marshal d'Estrées in the 99,000-man Army of the Lower Rhine. (It was in Germany that France committed the vast bulk of its regular land forces against the allied army composed of elements from Hanover, Hesse, Brunswick–Lüneburg, and England.) In 1761, still in Germany, he was promoted to brigadier general, and then to major general in 1762. Finally, in 1781, he was promoted to the highest military rank in France, that of lieutenant general. He died in Paris in 1796. (Crowley, "Surlaville," 444; Lee Kennett, *The French Armies in the Seven Years' War* [Durham, N.C.: Duke University Press, 1967], xiv.) Gaston Du Boscq de Beaumont (*Les derniers jours de l'Acadie 1748-1758: correspondances et mémoires* [Paris: 1899; reprint, Geneva: Slatkine-Megaroitis Reprints, 1975], 3) wrote that Surlaville was promoted to major general of the Army of the Lower Rhine in 1754. (The Archives du Séminaire de Québec has a collection of Surlaville papers in *Polygraphie,* nos. 55, 56, 57, and 58.)

The Crosses of Saint-Louis won by Surlaville and Raymond accompanied their being received into the Royal and Military Order of Saint-Louis. To be admitted to the order it was necessary that one be an officer in the regular troops, thereby excluding militia officers and enlisted men, and that one serve only the king of France (Marcel Trudel, *Initiation à la Nouvelle-France* [Montréal: Les éditions HRW ltée, 1971], 181).

10. See page 143 in Part IV of this work for the specific page references and details of Raymond's attempts within this document to improve his lot.

11. See Part IV for a comparative analysis of Raymond's original report and Surlaville's edited version.

12. The handwriting in *Pièce n° 35* differs from examples of Raymond's complete signature on several *actes notariés* examined by the present author. See notes 2, 3, and 4 in appendix 2 for further details on the manuscripts.

13. Letter to the present author from Roanne Mokhtar, reference archivist of the National Archives of Canada, 16 March 1993.

14. Cited in Yves F. Zoltvany, *The French Tradition in America* (Columbia: University of South Carolina Press, 1969), 127-30.

15. While France was required to give up Acadia, "with its ancient boundaries," those boundaries were ill-defined and construed differently by the British and the French. All or part of Acadia had changed hands many times between France and England since early in the seventeenth century. The political position taken by the French in 1713 was that Acadia consisted of only the peninsula of Nova Scotia, excluding the French-dominated mainland areas lying in what is now New Brunswick, the northern coast of Maine, and the southern coast of the Gaspé Peninsula. The British, however, never gave up their claim to the disputed Acadian territory beyond Nova Scotia. By the 1750s, prior to the Seven Years' War, they had strengthened their presence, both civil and military, on the peninsula and along the disputed borders.

    For an interesting discussion of the boundaries and geography of Acadia, see Andrew Hill Clark, *Acadia: The Geography of Early Nova Scotia to 1760* (Madison: University of Wisconsin Press, 1968), 71-74. See Eccles, *The Canadian Frontier*, 142, 172-73 for synopses of the role of the French-allied Abenaki and Micmac Indians who fought against the encroaching English settlers up to the Seven Years' War and the subsequent deportation of the French Acadian population in 1755. R. Cole Harris, ed., *Historical Atlas of Canada*, 3 vols. "From the Beginning to 1800" (Toronto: University of Toronto Press, 1987), 1:plate 30, provides a clear graphic and written account of the Acadian deportation.

16. The Louisiana colony was founded by Pierre Le Moyne d'Iberville and his younger brother, Jean-Baptiste Le Moyne de Bienville, in 1699. At first entirely dependent upon the Crown, Louisiana became a proprietary colony in 1712. By 1731 it was necessary for the desperately struggling colony to revert to Crown status for survival. In theory, the governor of Louisiana reported to the governor

general of New France in Quebec, but in reality the former reported to the minister of Marine, and through him to the king, as did his counterpart in Quebec.

The Carolina English, allied with and trading partners of the formidable Chickasaw nation, built a road from Charles Town to the latter's villages only some 100 miles east of the Mississippi where English traders flew their own flag when under fire from attacking French forces during the Chickasaw Wars. For the history of French Louisiana from 1698 to 1731, see Marcel Giraud, *Histoire de la Louisiane française*, 5 vols., (Paris: Presses universitaires de France, 1953-87). English translations of volumes 1, 2, and 5 have been published by the Louisiana State University Press (Baton Rouge, 1974, 1993, 1991). W. J. Eccles concisely treats the history of French Louisiana in his *France in America*, rev. ed. (East Lansing: Michigan State University Press, 1990), 157-87, and is a good source of information on the colony. Daniel H. Usner Jr.'s award-winning *Indians, Settlers, & Slaves in a Frontier Exchange Economy: The Lower Mississippi Valley before 1783* ([Chapel Hill: The University of North Carolina Press, 1992], 6) examines "the economic context in which different peoples continuously interacted with each other." The book's two parts analyze in fascinating detail the evolution of the region, and the social and commercial components of the "frontier exchange."

17. See Co-Intendant Antoine-Denis Raudot's detailed and farsighted recommendations of 1706 to Minister of Marine Jérôme Phélypeaux de Pontchartrain for the settlement and fortifying of Cape Breton Island, translated by Zoltvany, *The French Tradition in America*, 131-35; See also Eccles, *France in America*, 115. For fifteen highly informative essays on Louisbourg from 1713 to today, see Eric Krause, Carol Corbin, and William O'shea, eds., *Aspects of Louisbourg* (Sydney, Nova Scotia: University College of Cape Breton Press, 1995).

18. For an overview of the development and westward expansion of New France, see Eccles, *The Canadian Frontier*. Dale Miquelon's *New France 1701-1744: A Supplement to Europe* (Toronto: McClelland & Stewart, 1987) provides a perceptive analysis of the colony's history with valuable detail on economic and social development. For the development of French Louisiana, see chapter 6, "The Slave Colonies," in Eccles's *France in America*, 157-87. For a synopsis of the explorations for the Western Sea and the establishment of the French posts in the region, see the Introduction to Lawrence J. Burpee, ed., *Journals and Letters of Pierre Gaultier de Varennes de La Vérendrye and His Sons* (Toronto: Champlain Society, 1927), 1-40.

19. Minutes of the Council of Marine, Paris, 5 January 1718, AN Col., $C^{11}A$ 124: renumbered item no. 4, 9-10.

For a concise treatment of the mixed success of the Catholic missions among the Indians of New France, see Cornelius J. Jaenen, *The Role of the Church in New France*, Historical Booklet No. 40 (Ottawa: Canadian Historical Association, 1985), 9-11. See also chapter 2 of Jaenen's *Friend and Foe: Aspects of French-Amerindian Cultural Contact in the Sixteenth and Seventeenth Centuries* (Toronto: McClelland and Stewart, 1976), 41-83.

20. See Joseph L. Peyser, *Letters from New France: The Upper Country 1686-1783* (Urbana: University of Illinois Press, 1992), 36-38 for a discussion of this symbiotic relationship or "troika." For the accommodations developed between the French and the Indians, see Richard White, *The Middle Ground: Indians, Empires, and Republics in the Great Lakes Region* (Cambridge: Cambridge University Press, 1991). Also see W. J. Eccles, "Sovereignty Association, 1500-1783," *Canadian Historical Review* 65, no. 4 (December 1984): 475-510.

21. Projet de guerre contre les Renards, 1er octobre 1727 [misdated in the archives as 1737], AN Col., C^{11}A 67: 204r-204v.

For the diverse impact of the Oswego post on the Iroquois, see Francis Jennings, *Empire of Fortune: Crowns, Colonies, and Tribes in the Seven Years War in America* (New York: W. W. Norton & Co., 1988), 74-75; Francis Jennings, *Ambiguous Iroquois Empire: The Covenant Chain Confederation of Indian Tribes with English Colonies from Its Beginnings to the Lancaster Treaty of 1744* (New York: W. W. Norton & Co., 1984), 298-300; and Daniel K. Richter, *The Ordeal of the Longhouse: The Peoples of the Iroquois League in the Era of European Colonization* (Chapel Hill: University of North Carolina Press, 1992), 248-54. See also Johnson Gaylord Cooper, "Oswego in the French-English Struggle in North America" (Ph.D. diss., Syracuse University, 1961). The French finally captured Fort Oswego in 1756 during the Seven Years' War. The English reoccupied it in June 1759 as the war approached its end.

For examples of the vicious rivalry involving Oswego between the two colonial powers and a discussion of the hundreds of Miami Indian deaths from tainted Oswego brandy in the 1730s, see Peyser, *Letters from New France*, 135-46.

For details on the construction of Fort Niagara, see Brian Leigh Dunnigan, *Glorious Old Relic: The French Castle and Old Fort Niagara* (Youngstown, N.Y.: Old Fort Niagara Assoc., 1987) and Frank H. Severance, *An Old Frontier of France: The Niagara Region and Adjacent Lakes under French Control*, 2 vols. (New York: Dodd, Mead and Co., 1917), 1:227-38.

22. The success of the French in drawing furs away from the English at Hudson Bay by 1735 is described by Conrad E. Heidenreich and Françoise Noël as causing "a marked decline in the fur returns at Fort Albany and York Factory" (Harris, ed., *Historical Atlas of Canada*, 1:plate 39), and by Yves F. Zoltvany as "spectacular" ("Gaultier de Varennes et de La Vérendrye, Pierre," *DCB*, 3:251).

The Indian allies of the French against the Foxes at one time or another included the Ottawas, Potawatomis, Chippewas, Miamis, Piankeshaws, Illinois, Missouris, Hurons, Christian Iroquois (residing near Montreal), and Menominees; the Sauks and Ouiatanons fought with the French against the Foxes, but were sympathetic toward the latter.

The shifting alliances of a number of the tribes greatly affected the outcome of this and other wars involving the Indians and the European colonial powers. Until 1728 the Mascoutens and Kickapoos were allied with the Foxes, as were the Winnebagos until 1729, when, respectively, these nations joined the French. After the Foxes suffered two disastrous defeats in 1730 and 1732, the Sauks joined with them and together they successfully resisted the French until the latter pardoned both nations in 1737. These shifts were not arbitrary, having been precipitated in turn by unwise acts by both the Foxes and the French.

For full treatment of the French-Fox conflict, see R. David Edmunds and Joseph L. Peyser, *The Fox Wars: The Mesquakie Challenge to New France* (Norman: University of Oklahoma Press, 1993) and Joseph L. Peyser, "The Fate of the Fox Survivors: A Dark Chapter in the History of the French in the Upper Country, 1726-1737," *Wisconsin Magazine of History* 73 (winter 1989-90): 83-110.

23. For a concise picture of the conflict with the Chickasaws, see Joseph L. Peyser, "The Chickasaw Wars of 1736 and 1740: French Military Drawings and Plans Document the Struggle for the Lower Mississippi," *Journal of Mississippi History* 44 (February 1982): 1-25.

24. Blaine Adams, "Le Prévost Duquesnel (Du Quesnel), Jean-Baptiste," *DCB*, 3:392; Byron Fairchild, "Pepperrell, Sir William," *DCB*, 3:507-8; Eccles, *The Canadian Frontier*, 150-53.

25. The staggering loss of the French fleet and accompanying army under the Duke d'Anville is vividly brought to life by James Pritchard in his superlative *Anatomy of a Naval Disaster: The 1746 French Expedition to North America* (Montreal and Kingston: McGill-Queen's University Press, 1995). See William A. Hunter's articles "Orontony (Orontondi, Rondoenie, Wanduny, Nicolas)," *DCB*, 3:495-96, for details on the Huron leader of the revolt, and "Tanaghrisson (Deanaghrison, Johonerissa, Tanacharison, Tanahisson, Thanayieson and, as a title, the Half King)," *DCB*, 3:613-14, on the Seneca leader of the Ohio Iroquois (Mingo) who closely cooperated with Croghan to subvert the Miami. See also Michael N. McConnell, *A Country Between: The Upper Ohio Valley and Its Peoples, 1724-1774* (Lincoln: University of Nebraska Press, 1992).

26. Mémoire sur les Sauvages du Canada, Versailles, le 28 janvier 1748, AN Col., $C^{11}E$ 13:162-63 recto. This document provides details on the Huron Conspiracy; it is translated in its entirety in Peyser, *Jacques Legardeur de Saint-Pierre*, 102-4; both chapters 3 and 4 contain newly translated documents relating to the Huron Conspiracy, referred to as "a general conspiracy of the black skins against the white" by Montreal Governor Dubois Berthelot (Mémoire de Dubois Berthelot, Montréal, novembre 1747, AN Col., $C^{11}A$ 87:16). His dramatic description of the Indian tactics and the fear experienced by the French is translated in Peyser, *Letters from New France*, 184-85.

For an excellent analytical overview (from the 1740s to 1754) of the economic and military struggles of the French and English to win over the Indians of the Ohio Valley (and those of the more westerly nations), see Pease and Jenison, *IHC*, 29:xix-lii.

27. W. J. Eccles, "Céloron de Blainville, Pierre-Joseph," *DCB*, 3:100; Eccles, *The Canadian Frontier*, 159; Joseph Cossette, "Bonnécamps, Joseph-Pierre de," *DCB*, 4:76-77. The French transcript and English translation of Bonnécamps's report to La Galissonière are published in Reuben Gold Thwaites, ed., "Relation du voyage de la Belle Rivière fait en 1749, sous les ordres de M. de Céloron, par le P. Bonnecamps," *Jesuit Relations and Allied Documents*, 73 vols. (New York: Pageant Book Co., 1959), 69:150-99. An English translation of Céloron's journal is "1749: Céloron's Expedition down the Ohio," Reuben Gold Thwaites, ed., *Collections of the State Historical Society of Wisconsin* (hereafter cited as *WHC*), 20 vols. (Madison: Society, 1854-1911), 18:36-58.

28. Compte Général du produit des Postes des pays d'en haut et de la dépense Sur ce produit, Québec, le 17 septembre 1749, AN Col., C¹¹A 116:145 recto-145 verso. This trading post was located on the White River to the south and west of the main Miami post. The entry is translated in full in Peyser, *Jacques Legardeur de Saint-Pierre*, 88.

29. These are my translations of Copies des lettres de M. de Raymond, Commandant aux Miamis, écrites à M. le Marquis de La Jonquière, aux Miamis le 4 et le 5 7bre 1749, National Archives of Canada (hereafter cited as NAC), MG1, AN Col., C¹¹A, 93:66-68, 69-71. These letters were also translated and published in *IHC*, 29:105-8, 108-11.

30. Nicolas, a Huron chief also known as Orontony, settled near Sandoské (Sandusky) Bay in an area under the influence of English traders. In August 1747 he was implicated in the deaths of a number of Frenchmen in the Miami country and later near Detroit, where he was talking peace with the French. When Detroit was reinforced in late September 1747, Nicolas and 119 of his warriors left for the Ohio Valley, nearer the English (Hunter, "Orontony," *DCB*, 3:495-96). The three forts, the swivel guns, and the mortars reported here as fact by Raymond were undoubtedly rumor in what Pease and Jenison called an "alarmist report." In view of independent confirmation of the dangerous situation from the Illinois commandant, however, they later justified Raymond's alarms (*IHC*, 29:xxxi, xxxix).

31. Coldfoot, *Pied froid* in French, was loyal to the French. He and many Miami remained at the French post where he tried to neutralize La Demoiselle's influence. He was not at the post when some of La Demoiselle's Miami killed several French there.

32. Probably Louis-Jacques-Charles Renaud Dubuisson. He was a full ensign at this time. See *WHC*, 17:457, 460, 468, 505-6; and André Lachance, "Renaud Dubuisson, Louis-Jacques-Charles," *DCB*, 3:551.

33. The year after he was recalled from the Miami post in 1750, Raymond wrote to the minister to complain that he should not have been replaced there. Neither he nor his successor, Louis Coulon de Villiers, who commanded the post until 1753, enjoyed much success in the assignment. See *WHC*, 18:94-98 for the translation

of Raymond's letter. Governor General Duquesne was clearly not happy with the two officers' service in the turbulent Miami country: he withheld Villiers's extra pay for his last two years as commandant of the Miami post (Villiers to the minister, Montreal, 9 October 1754, An Col., C¹¹E 13:221-22).

34. *WHC*, 18:58-60; *IHC*, 29:119-31, 149-56, 166-216, passim. For transcripts and translations of the correspondence to and from Raymond while he commanded the Miami post, see *IHC*, 29:163-216.

35. Raymond to La Jonquière, the Miami post, 14 May 1750, NAC MG1, AN Col., C¹¹A 95: transcript p. 352, translation by the present author. The complete letter and enclosed reports are transcribed and translated in *IHC*, 29:188-200.

36. Raymond to La Jonquière, the Miami post, 22 May 1750, NAC MG1, AN Col., C¹¹A 95: transcript p. 365, translated by the present author. The entire letter is transcribed and translated in *IHC*, 29:201-16.

37. The highest rank held by an officer of the *Troupes de la Marine* was that of captain. The administration of each of the fortified towns of Quebec, Montreal, and Trois-Rivières was composed of a town governor and his military staff. Under the governor were the *lieutenant de roi* (king's lieutenant, functioning as lieutenant-governor), the *major* (town major), and the *aide-major* (town adjutant).

La Jonquière exceptionally appointed Céloron as major, even though Detroit did not have the status of a town. Although his rank in the *Troupes de la Marine* remained that of captain, his title of major was nonetheless viewed by the *Marine* officers and others as a superior rank. See, for example, Voucher from Delisle to La Jonquière, Detroit, 3 September 1750, AN Col., C¹¹A 119:263, in which the merchant refers to Céloron as "Monsieur de Céloron, major in command at this place." In Raymond to Rouillé, 1 October 1751, NAC microfilm C2399, AN Col., C¹¹A 97: transcript p. 304, Raymond entreats the minister *de luy accorder la Commission de Major Commandant de Missilimaquinac* ("to grant him the commission of major in command of Michilimackinac"), a suggestion he reiterates in his *dénombrement* to Surlaville (NAC 2951 in Part III). For explanations of Canadian staff ranks and ranks in the *Troupes de la Marine*, see Trudel, *Initiation à la Nouvelle-France*, 172-77, and Chartrand, *Canadian Military Heritage*, 1:107-8.

38. La Jonquière's orders to Villiers, Montreal, 10 July 1750, AN Col., C¹¹E 13:194, transcribed and translated in *IHC*, 29:217-23. La Jonquière was to be disappointed in both Céloron and Villiers, neither one being able to quell the disturbances in the Miami country.

Villiers was born at Verchères, Québec, in 1710. In 1725 his father was assigned to the Saint Joseph River post (Fort Saint Joseph, now Niles, Michigan). According to Dunning Idle and to a 1725 map drawn by Chaussegros de Léry, the chief engineer of New France, there were both Potawatomi and Miami villages at the post (Jean-Guy Pelletier, "Coulon de Villiers, Nicolas-Antoine," *DCB*, 2:156; W. J. Eccles, "Coulon de Villiers, Louis," *DCB*, 3:148; Dunning Idle, "The Post of the St. Joseph River during the French Régime 1679-1761"

[Ph.D. diss., University of Illinois, 1946], 153, 160-63; Recueil No 67, Carte N°
15, Service historique de la Marine, Vincennes).

39. Villiers to the minister, Montreal, 9 October 1754, AN Col., C¹¹E 13:221-22,
    translated in *Letters from New France*, 209-10; *WHC*, 18:20f, 110; W. J. Eccles,
    "Céloron de Blainville, Pierre-Joseph," *DCB*, 3:100; Paul Trap, "Mouet de
    Langlade, Charles-Michel," *DCB*, 4:563. See *WHC*, 18:104-17 for a translation
    of Acting Governor General Charles Le Moyne de Longueuil's 21 April 1752
    report to the minister on the "sorrowful condition" of the upper country. Bigot
    to the minister, Quebec, 4 November 1752 (statement of expenses for the *pays
    d'en haut* 1752), AN Col., C¹¹A 119:310 recto-311 verso, and *WHC*, 18:128-32
    provide details on Langlade's raid on Pickawillany. Two of the English traders
    hid during Langlade's attack and escaped capture.
40. Minister to Duquesne, Versailles, 31 May 1754, AN Col., B 99:199-200.
41. Pierre-L. Côté, "Duquesne (Du Quesne, Duqaine, Duquêne) de Menneville,
    Ange, Marquis Duquesne," *DCB*, 4:256. For a detailed account of Bigot's career
    and malversations in New France, see J. F. Bosher and J.-C. Dubé, "Bigot,
    François," *DCB*, 4:59-71.
42. Eccles, *The Canadian Frontier*, 160-62; Eccles, "Marin de La Malgue (La Marque),
    Paul," *DCB*, 3:431-32; Côté, "Duquesne," *DCB*, 4:256; *The Journal of Major
    George Washington*, facsimile ed. (Williamsburg: Colonial Williamsburg
    Foundation, 1959), 13.
43. Peyser, *Jacques Legardeur de Saint-Pierre*, 205-6; see chapter 7 for Saint-Pierre's
    complete letter as well as other previously untranslated letters by Duquesne,
    Saint-Pierre, and other French officers stationed in the Ohio Valley in 1753-54.
44. Ibid., 206-12; Eccles, *The Canadian Frontier*, 163-64.
45. For an English translation of Louis Coulon de Villiers's journal of his campaign
    against Washington, including the controversial Fort Necessity surrender terms,
    see Peyser, *Letters from New France*, 198-208. In his journal, Villiers identified the
    Indians of his contingent as Hurons, Abenakis, Christian Iroquois, Nepissings,
    Algonquins, and Ottawas, all living at Fort Duquesne (*Letters*, 198-99). See
    Eccles's *The Canadian Frontier*, 159-67, for an excellent account of the developing
    confrontation in the Ohio Valley.
46. Minister to Duquesne, Versailles, 31 May 1754, AN Col., B 99:199-200.
47. Duquesne to Minister, Quebec, 7 October 1754, AN Col. C¹¹A 99:257 (trans-
    lated on p. 4 of this work); Côté, "Duquesne," *DCB*, 4:256-57.

II. ABOUT THE TRANSLATION

Raymond's writing in his *dénombrement* is in many respects quite typical of eighteenth-century writings by officers of the *Troupes de la Marine* in Canada. The fact that the "original" is in this case actually a beautifully penned copy made in 1754 by a professional writer virtually eliminates problems arising from poor handwriting. Even so, I had to be alert for Raymond's stylistic idiosyncracies, including: (1) a myriad of aberrant spellings such as *quant resulte il?* for *qu'en résulte-t-il?*, *son* for *sans*, *ses* for *ces*, *chartiers* for *charretiers*, *pourcelines* for *porcelaine*, *Herrier* for *Erié*, *Ste Clere* for *Sainte-Claire*, *8ÿatanons* for *Ouiatanons*, and *yrocois* for *Iroquois*; (2) convoluted and run-on sentences sometimes a page in length; (3) missing or inappropriate punctuation; and (4) frequent lapses in grammar such as incorrect agreement of subject and verb, confusion of the spelling of the past participle and the second person plural of the present tense, incorrect sequence of tenses, omission of the *ne* in negations, lack of parallel construction, and misuse of the imperfect subjunctive.

Another challenge was the identification and location of places with obsolete names in the vast territories described by Raymond, and the identification of individuals mentioned, including several whose names were misspelled, who are known today by other names, or whose names were omitted entirely by Raymond. Familiarity with eighteenth-century military, commercial, religious, and other terms, including symbols and abbreviations in use at the time, was also needed.

Raymond's *dénombrement* was admittedly unpolished; on his first page he wrote, "Do not expect a polished report with each word weighed as if it were to be placed under the eyes of a minister." It is a document written by someone who had spent his adult life on the frontier, with few demands for precision in grammar, spelling, and rhetoric. As a result, I

43

found it a more challenging but more enjoyable and colorful document to translate than the official version carefully crafted in Surlaville's office.

My goal was to render an accurate and readable English-language equivalent of the manuscript that would retain the flavor of the original. Achieving readability and retaining the original flavor are often conflicting goals in translating documents written by eighteenth-century North American French frontier authors. Raymond's run-on sentences on occasion fill an entire legal-size page; to preserve this characteristic is to lose readability. Therefore, I generally reduced such passages to manageable sentences, adding punctuation and making minor but necessary changes in wording. At the same time, I retained the author's lengthy paragraphs and some of his aberrant spellings in order to convey something of the flavor and structure of the original. Upon the suggestion of a number of the National Endowment for the Humanities readers of sample translated passages, I used modern capitalization throughout in order to avoid distracting today's reader of the English version.

Retaining the original flavor—both in transcribing and translating—has not always been in vogue. Pierre Margry (*Découvertes et établissements des Français dans l'ouest et dans le sud de l'Amérique septentrionale* [*1614-1754*], 6 vols., Paris: Maisonneuve et Cie, 1879-88), for example, and Aegidius Fauteux to a lesser extent have consciously sought to improve the literary level of the originals in their published transcriptions. Margry at times even extensively rewrote and made major changes in the documents. The same tendency is seen in many translators, as, for example, in Edith Moodie's elegant unpublished translations of Margry's transcripts.[1] However, I chose to cleave more closely to the original, as indicated above.

I also attempted to avoid translations that are too literal, where the result is unnatural or stilted English. As an example, Raymond asked, *Comment pourroit on faire des fortunes si rapides Si on Egorgoit* [*sic*] *pas la bourse du Roy?* (NAC transcript, page 2969), which I rendered as "How could they make such quick fortunes if they were not dipping into the king's purse?" A literal (and unacceptable) translation of Raymond's metaphor would be "if they were not cutting (the throat of) the king's purse." Preserving the literalness of both portions of the metaphor in English is awkward, as in "if they were not bleeding the king's purse." The mundane "if they were not stealing the king's money" conveys the meaning and is good English, but it departs completely from the metaphor and loses all of the imagery of the original. I was tempted to use an equivalent English expression, "if they were not picking the king's pocket," but ultimately decided to retain half of the metaphor ("the king's purse") and to use figuratively and colloquially the English verb "to dip" in place of the equally colloquial use of the French *égorger*. Thus, a coherent English metaphor preserves both the sense and something of the flavor of Raymond's original.

Generally, I corrected Raymond's irregular syntax and spelling (preserving some irregularities for color) in my translation but always sought to convey the precise thoughts of the author. Where any ambiguity existed, it was noted. The annotations include: (1) explanations of archaic, obsolete, and specialized terms; (2) notes on inconsistencies, variations, and problems within the text; (3) bibliographic references to allow the reader to obtain additional information on particular points; (4) identifications of individuals mentioned or referred to in the text; (5) identifications of places with obsolete names; (6) related citations from other manuscripts or publications; and (7) historical background for events mentioned in the text. A few of these annotations are of substantial length, particularly those providing biographical information on people named and historical context. For example, this information will help distinguish between members of large families who have similar names and who have been confused with one another, often the case with officers of the *Troupes de la Marine*.

For the reader of this translation who may wish to refer to particular corresponding sections of the unpublished French versions of the document, the beginning of each of the original folio pages is indicated in this translation in boldface by a number followed by an **r** for recto or a **v** for verso in the margin, e.g. **151r, 151v**. The National Archives of Canada pagination is indicated in the margin by the letters NAC and the transcript page number, e.g., NAC 2943, which mark the beginning of that transcript page.

The few significant differences between the original of the Raymond *dénombrement* in Paris and the NAC transcript are noted in the translation. Several observations are also noted regarding Fauteux's transcript. Because of the corrections and modifications in this transcript, I have made only infrequent reference to it. However, the reader who is not comfortable with eighteenth-century handwritten French may find Fauteux's modernized version useful in light of the fact that it does not make any substantive change from the original.

As a typical French colonial officer in the mid-eighteenth century, Raymond used only the noun *Anglais* in referring to the English, British, or Anglo-Americans. The French synonym *Britannique*, meaning "Briton" or "Britisher," was scarcely used by the French North American colonists.

Even as an adjective, *britannique* was reserved by the French for formal use, as in treaties. While the noun *Anglais* can correctly be translated as "Englishman," "Briton," or "Britisher" in the singular, and "English(men)" or "British" in the plural, and the adjective *anglais* as "English" or "British," I have for the most part used the words "English" and "Englishmen" thoughout this book in order to be consistent with Raymond's usage, perception, and time frame.[2]

Boldface type is used in the translation where Raymond used bold letters. The original spelling of place names and of individuals' names has been retained for the most part. The first time used, however, they are followed by brackets containing alternate eighteenth-century French spellings and the modern English equivalent.

Surlaville (or perhaps Raymond) underlined six lengthy portions of the *dénombrement*. It appears that these sections were to be limited to Surlaville's eyes only, not to be presented to the new minister of Marine, Jean-Baptiste Machault d'Arnouville. These marked pages reveal the dishonesty, self-seeking, or poor administration on the part of various officers, government officials, or members of the clergy in New France. The underlining is not reproduced in the translation, but the beginning of each such section is marked with a single boldface asterisk (*****) and the end of each is marked with double boldface asterisks (******). The six sections are as follows, identified by their original folio page numbers and, in parentheses, by their NAC transcript page numbers:

> Folio pages 139 verso - 140 verso (NAC 2907-9)
> Folio pages 148 recto - 150 recto (NAC 2928-33)
> Folio pages 159 recto - 160 verso (NAC 2954-58)
> Folio pages 163 recto - 164 recto (NAC 2964-67)
> Folio pages 165 recto - 166 recto (NAC 2970-72)
> Folio pages 169 recto - 169 verso (NAC 2980-81)

NOTES

1. Copies of Moodie's translations are in the Library of Michigan in Lansing, the Burton Historical Collection of the Detroit Public Library, and the University of Chicago Library.
2. Linda Colley examines the "profound uncertainty about the workings of the imperial relationship" between the Thirteen Colonies and the mother country in her *Britons: Forging the Nation 1707-1837* (New Haven, Conn.: Yale University

Press, 1992). She posits (135) the "conflicting images" of "Americans as colonists subordinate to the mother country [and] *Americans as Englishmen abroad and consequently brethren of those at home* . . . [emphasis added]." She cites (136) John Adams's 1775 statement that "The two realms of England and Scotland were, by the Act of Union, incorporated into one kingdom by the name of Great Britain; but there is not one word about America in that Act." If on the eve of the Seven Years' War many Anglo-Americans thought of themselves as English rather than as British, it is reasonable that their Franco-American neighbors thought of them as English as well.

Although a case can be made for the use of "British" for *Anglais* in the present study, I prefer the use of "Englishmen." In the same way, I have translated Raymond's *Français* as "Frenchmen" even though one might say that he was writing about Canadians.

III. ANNOTATED TRANSLATION OF <u>LE DÉNOMBREMENT DE TOUS LES POSTES DU CANADA</u>

I

I must satisfy you, then, my dear sur La ville [Surlaville],[1] and give NAC 2895 you as you wish <u>the enumeration of all the posts of Canada</u>, the places 135r where they are located, those where the king keeps garrisons which are the keys to the country, those that are trading posts, the present upkeep of the garrisons, the posts, the commanders of these various posts, what can be done better than what is being done in them up to now to hold on to the various Indian nations and to deprive them of the opportunity to go to the English. Do not expect a polished report with each word weighed as if it were to be placed under the eyes of a minister, but you can count on the truth such as it is without disguise, without dissimulation, without bias and, even more, without respect for the individual. There are many things in it that I would have to suppress if I had the honor of speaking to the minister.[2] You asked me for the truth; I am telling it to you as a gentleman, as a Christian. That is why I am allowing you to submit this report, which I am only doing for you, to the scrutiny of all those who know Canada as completely as I have had good reason to know it during the past 32 years during which I have had the honor of serving His Majesty there. The various commands that the generals have entrusted to me as you have seen from their orders with which they provided me, that is what has given me NAC 2896 a general knowledge of this country, and of the Indians, and of the general background for everything that involves or concerns the service and the country. 135v

Enumeration of the posts in the extent of the general governance of Canada where the officers of the troops go in command, provided with orders from the generals who select them.

First page of Charles de Raymond's *dénombrement de tous les postes du Canada,*
1754. *Reproduced with permission of the Archives de Saint-Sulpice, Paris; from manu-*
scrit 1200, pièce 35 of the collection "Pièces pour l'histoire militaire du Canada 1730-
1760."

POSTS OF THE NORTH

1. Themiskamingues [Témiscamingues; Temiscaming];[3] no commandant is assigned there.
2. Michilimaquinac [Michilimakinac; Missilimakinak, etc.; Michilimackinac; Mackinaw City, Michigan]
3. La Baye [Green Bay, Wisconsin][4]
4. La mer du Ouest [La mer de l'Ouest; The Western Sea][5]
5. Le Sault Ste. Marie, granted as a seigneury with exclusive trading to Sieur de Bonne,[6] in perpetuity to him and to his family.
6. Cha8amigon [Chagouamigon; La Pointe; Ashland, Wisconsin][7]
7. Kamanistigouya [Kaministigoya; Kaministiquia; Thunder Bay, Ontario]
8. Nopigond [Népigon; Nipigon, Ontario][8]
9. Michypicotton [Michipicoton; Michipicoten]; no commandant is assigned there[9]
10. St. Joseph [le poste de la rivière Saint-Joseph; le fort de Saint-Joseph; Niles, Michigan][10]
11. The Illinois River. Until now, no commandant has been assigned there. The general sells congés to the traders to trade there with the Indians.[11]

    Leaving Montreal, the route for going to these posts is via the   NAC 2897
    Grande Rivière [Ottawa River].[12] They are located on Lakes Huron, Michigan, and Superior. The river of the Illinois bears the name of the Indians of this name and flows into the Mississipi [*sic*].

POSTS IN THE SOUTHERN PART

12. La Présentation [Ogdensburg, New York]. A useless post on the Frontenac River [Catarakoui River; the upper St. Lawrence River] 40 leagues[13] above Montreal. Newly established at the instigation of the Abbé Piquet [Picquet]. There are many observations to be made and many things to be said about this post, especially the great expenditures that the king has made there and that it is presently causing.[14]
13. Fort Frontenac [Cataracoui; Kingston, Ontario] at the entrance of   136r
    Lake Ontario.

14. Fort Toronteaux [Fort Rouillé; Toronto, Ontario], a new post on Lake Ontario to the northwest of this lake.

15. Niagara at the other end of Lake Ontario [at Youngstown, New York, 14 miles north of the falls].

16. Detroit on the river which takes the discharge from Lakes Huron and St. Clair and which flows into Lake Erie which flows into Lake Ontario through Niagara Falls.

17. The Miami [Fort Wayne, Indiana], 60 leagues in the south above Detroit on the little Miami River which flows into Lake Erie.

18. The 8ÿatanon [Ouiatanon; Ouyatanon, etc.; West Lafayette, Indiana], 60 leagues above the Miami on the Wabash River.

NAC 2898   The posts which are beyond come under the Mississipi government.[15]

19. The Presqu'ile Post [Erie, Pennsylvania]
20. The Duquesne Post [Pittsburgh, Pennsylvania]
21. The Rivière au Boeuf Post [Fort Le Boeuf; Waterford, Pennsylvania]

[These last three are] new posts established on the Belle Rivière [Ohio River] in 1753 and 1754.

The route for going to these posts leaving from Montreal is via the Frontenac River which the Indians call the Catarakouy. This river is formed by the discharge from the above-named lakes. It is enlarged by several other rivers which come out of the north and south lands and which flow into it.

22. Chambly is above the Chambly River [Richelieu River] and below the discharge of Lake Champlain.[16]

23. St. Jean is a new post established on Lake Champlain used as an entrepôt for Fort St. Frédéric [Crown Point, New York].

24. Fort St. Frédéric, established at the end of Lake Champlain,[17] which is near the English of Fort Sarasteaux [Saratoga, New York; now Schuylerville, New York], Orange [Albany, New York], and Corlac [Corlear, Corlar; Schenectady, New York], located in New England in the region called Albany. One can also go to the English via Lake St. Sacrement [Lake George, New York] near Fort St. Frédéric to the west of this fort, taking the portage named after this lake which is beautiful and easy. One can take this route by canoe and by bateau.[18] One can also have them pass through this portage to reach

136v

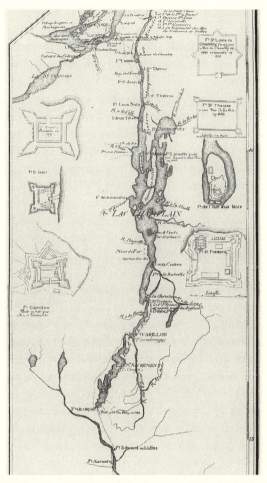

French forts in the Lake Champlain region, ca. 1758. The French forts listed by Raymond and several of the English forts are shown in this curious composite map dating from several time periods.   The basic map of the Lake Champlain region, most of which is shown here, was drawn in 1752 by Franquet. Other features were added later, including Fort Carillon (Ticonderoga; built in 1755). This is one of five early maps added to the borders of a modern map of New France (published in 1875). *Detail from the Carte du Lac Champlain, de la Riv. des Iroquois et de l'Isle de Montréal by Franquet, 1752, this map being inserted in the border of the Carte de la Nouvelle France pour servir à l'étude de l'histoire du Canada, depuis sa découverte jusqu'en 1760, by P.M.A. Genest, Burland-Desbarats, Montréal, 1875. Reproduced with permission, Musée de la civilisation, Fonds d'archives du Séminaire de Québec, T-219, no. 13, P-3, photographe Denis Chalfour.*

the river [i.e., the Hudson River] which goes to Sarasteaux and Orange.

At Chambly, in peacetime only one junior officer with one sergeant are necessary to guard it.

At St. Jean and at La Présentation only junior officers are needed as commandants and only 10 soldiers in each one in peacetime.

At Laprairie, at Sault St. Louis [Caugnawaga; Kahnawake, Quebec], at the Lac des Deux Montagnes [Lake of Two Mountains; Oka, Quebec][19] it is useless to keep commandants and troops there in peacetime because it needlessly increases expenses.

An observation to be made on the selection of the commandants who should be used and what results from this choice.

I observe that for the greatest advantage and the greatest good of the king's service, and in order to continually rekindle diligence, zeal, and emulation, only the captains should be employed for the command of these posts, officers who certainly from their long years of service have acquired more understanding, more knowledge, and more experience for leading and governing the Indian nations and the French who trade with them than the junior officers most of whom are but newcomers to the service. To prepare good officers it would be appropriate that the junior officers serve as second-in-command under the orders of the captains.

Otherwise the good order of the service is overturned. Have the generals[20] followed this rule up to now? Surely not. As they are despotic masters, they would never believe that they could make their power felt more than by making awards through favoritism, through intrigue, through solicitation. To whom then do they most often and almost always award these posts? To young men without experience or leadership. (As you know no one in Canada) I shall repeat what those who are without principle or respect for the individual demonstrate: that their advancement is obtained thanks to their pretty wives and female relatives. Husbands, brothers, relatives of these [women] favorites, these are the officers to whom these commands are given.[21] They are also given to those who know how to speak only the language of gold, or to those who ask for financial participation with them. And it is in these partnerships that things take place that prejudice the king's interests and the good of the colony that no one would dare bring to light. I repeat then that it is these officers to whom these commands are entrusted. Their dearth of experience, their greed to become rich result in these officers taking no interest whatever in the service, neglecting it entirely, and working only toward making their fortune during their preferential treatment, and that is what brought about a great deal of trouble and much disloyalty among the Indians at many posts during this last war.[22]

What has resulted from this? And what is resulting from this? Our NAC 2901 Indians, disgusted and dissatisfied, are taking their furs to the English, are becoming attached to them to the prejudice of our interests and to the detriment of the trade. This disgust on the part of the Indians comes from 137v their sovereign scorn of the officers whom they see fur trading with them. They no longer look upon them but as trading-goods chiefs, as they call them, and lose even more the confidence they would have in them, and no longer listen to them on those occasions when needed by the service, convinced as they are that the goods that they trade to them were sent as presents (by the Great Onontio whom they call their father[23]). In that they are not mistaken. The presents that the king has given to them to keep them loyal to him are not distributed to them. If any are given to them, they are mere trinkets; a profit is made from these presents. The Indians who are deprived of them contrary to their expectations leave the French to attach themselves only to the English whom they apprise of this behavior and who give them much in order to profit from the situation and to attract them, and that is what they have succeeded in doing and the Indians make much of this generosity from the English.

It is to be noted that the Indians are self-interested and attach them- NAC 2902 selves only to the one who gives them the most, and that they like the benefactor only through the benefit that they receive and expect from him. It is therefore an absolute necessity not only to give them the presents that the king gives them, but to give them moreover in their need, and to reward them well for the least little service rendered if it is desired that they serve you for the needs of the service. If they fail to be rewarded one single time, the good that was done for them before counts for nothing. The diplomacy and care that are necessary to keep them faithful are incredible, because they are distrustful, vindictive, traitorous, perfidious, 138r changeable, suspicious. That is why every care that a commandant must employ in order to serve usefully should attract the confidence of the Indians where he is in command. In order to succeed, he must be affable; appear to share their feelings; be generous without prodigality; always give them something, especially to their children; give them precisely the presents that are sent to him to be given to them; distribute them appropriately, as upon the occasions when they are needed for the service or to

Portrait of Louis XV ("The Great Onontio"), king of France, 1715–74.
Studio of Louis-Michel van Loo (1707–1771), after 1761. Reproduced with permission of the National Archives of Canada, C-604.

The Indians giving a Talk to Colonel Bouquet in a Conference at a Council Fire, near his Camp on the Banks of Muskingum in North America, in Oct. 1764.

Indian council with British officers, 1764.   *Benjamin West, artist, in William Smith,* A Historical Account of the Expedition Against the Ohio Indians in the Year 1764, under the Command of Henry Bouquet (1765). *Courtesy William L. Clements Library, University of Michigan.*

prevent them from going to the English. In giving them these presents,
NAC 2903 let it always be in the name of the Great Onontio,[24] chief of all the
French whom they call their father, and emphasize greatly what is being
given to them while maintaining their hope that they will always be
given more, but that this will only be in proportion to their giving [the
commandant] reason to be pleased with them and being docile in hearing
the speeches of their father and faithful in obeying him and doing his
will.

Knowing how to lead the Indians well and becoming their master is a
talent that you would not believe, difficult to acquire. All officers do not
succeed in it. It is acquired only in studying their character, their customs,
their passions, their nature, their tastes, their way of thinking, of expressing
themselves in their speeches. They are all metaphorical and allegorical[25]
and ordinarily reflect what they decided and resolved in councils held in
138v the past by their ancients with Messrs de Frontenac, Callière, and
Vaudreuil who were among the first generals of Canada.[26] From father to
son, the children know by tradition the agreements that their forefathers
made. Their official records are wampum belts[27] that they give and receive
to record forever with the same force as a contract the agreements and
NAC 2904 treaties that are made with them. Within each nation these belts constitute
their archives and are kept in depositories by one among them who is
chosen and named for that only, and when they come to speak of matters
that relate to what they have dealt with in the past, they bring out the
belts and repeat what was agreed upon by means of these belts, and ask
that their [present] speech—which is the belt that they give through
which they speak—be brought back [by the visitors].

The attention of an officer who is in command among the Indian
nations must therefore enter into the sense, the spirit of their thought. He
must be able to penetrate the metaphorical and allegorical meaning with
which they express themselves and to answer them using the same expression and the same style, take care to keep their belts and to send them to
the general with the Indians' speeches and the replies he gave them. This
is what must not be expected from young men, almost all without experience and who have no knowledge other than the preferential treatment of
which I have spoken. It is necessary for you to know also that after having
spoken or replied, that [sic] for each subject that you deal with you back it
up with a belt. The Indians do the same thing; we do it because the way
the Indians act with us is the way they do it among themselves. After the
NAC 2905 council is finished the commandant gives a present to the chiefs who

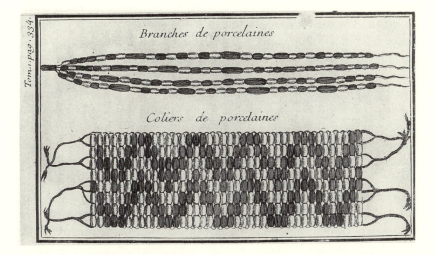

Branches de porcelaines

Coliers de porcelaines

Tom·pag·334·

Wampum strings and belts, 1722. *Reproduced from Bacqueville de La Potherie,* **Histoire de l'Amérique septentrionale** *(1722). Courtesy William L. Clements Library, the University of Michigan.*

made up the council. It [the gift] is always in proportion to the number in   **139r**
the assemblage and in the village and to the importance of the matters that
you have dealt with. It is in this way that an officer concerned for the
good of the service conducts himself. Should one expect this behavior
from these favored people? Undoubtedly not. And I will say, to their
shame, that most, if not all, make it appear on such occasions and on many
others that they have given substantial presents to the Indians, whereas
they gave them nothing or a mere trifle. They make their profit from what
they make it appear that they have given.[28] I would have so many similar
things to bring to light that it is better to omit them silently in order for
you to note **that Michilimaquinac** is the entrepôt of all the posts of the
northern region, just as Detroit is the entrepôt of all those which are
above Fort Niagara in the southern region.[29]

 I note the beauty of the climate of Detroit; the goodness and fertility
of the lands on which, in most of them, there is but little clearing to be
done; the quantity of grassland for raising as much livestock of all kinds as
one would like; the abundance of fishing and hunting; its proximity to the
posts of the Miami [and] Ouyatanon, which is [*sic*] the link with the

NAC 2906 Illinois country and the Mississipy via the Miami and Wabash Rivers; the link with and closeness of the new posts of the Belle Rivière which is only about one hundred leagues from Filadelfile [Philadelphia] by land and whose road is cleared by the continual comings and goings of the English who up to now have been doing the trading of this whole region, which

139v it is to be feared they will invade subsequently.

All these considerations, then, warrant our paying greater attention to Detroit than we have until now. Let us pour settlers into it in order to populate it and make it capable of protecting and feeding itself and the new settlements of the Belle Rivière in order to keep possession of them and keep our communications open with the Illinois and the Mississipy, in order to succeed and protect all those regions and your [sic] habitants, to assure them of a refuge to enable them not to lose their possessions and families with respect to the wars that we should always fear having with the English, or with the Indian nations. If we come to having it with the latter there is no holding onto Detroit if it remains in the situation it is in; its loss will certainly lead to that of all the regions of which we have just

NAC 2907 spoken, which obviously proves that it is appropriate to establish a town there, to have a governor there, a staff headquarters, and troops proportionate to the interest we must have in our expansion and in maintaining ourselves in such a good and beautiful region.[30]

For the peaceful and tranquil possession of all of Canada we have but two objects which warrant and must have the attention of the government, which is [sic] Detroit and the Belle Rivière of which I have just spoken, Isle Royale [Cape Breton Island, Nova Scotia], Acadia, and the Bay of Gaspé. Those regions are Canada's gateway. As for Acadia and Gaspé what important and interesting truths there would be to bring to light; I am omitting the knowledge I have of them in silence. ★My reflections on this subject would provide the material for a report were I to bring it to light. The court only listens, cares about, and pays attention to what comes from generals and intendants, assuming they have, because of hav-

140r ing chosen them, sufficient dedication to the service and a sufficiently large extent of knowledge and intelligence, extending over all the areas of knowledge that they ought to have and acquire from the regions they govern, for them to do what would be suitable there for their [the regions'] preservation. However all appearances are that the English will become masters of Acadia and the Gaspé which they are on the verge of settling.

NAC 2908   You have seen Acadia and the damaging error made by a commandant of La Baye Verte [Baie Verte, New Brunswick],[31] whom you know, not to

Map of the Detroit River from Lake Erie to Lake St. Clair, by Chaussegros de Léry, *fils*, 1752. Pierre-Joseph Céloron de Blainville was town major of Detroit when this map was drawn. The fort was located on the north side of the river, to the west of the Isle aux Cochons (Belle Isle). There were about 600 settlers at this time. Note that the land grants are at right angles to the river and are long and narrow, like those in the St. Lawrence Valley. *Carte de La Rivière du détroit depuis le Lac Erie jusques au Lac Ste. Claire, by Chaussegros de Léry, fils, 1752, Service historique de la Marine, Recueil 67, n° 71. Reproduced with permission; photograph courtesy of National Archives of Canada Ph/902/1752.*

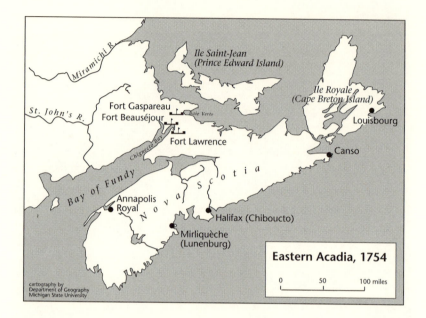

Eastern Acadia, 1754. **Fort Beauséjour faced Fort Lawrence, built by the British near the abandoned French settlement of Beaubassin. The French had to supply Fort Beauséjour overland from Fort Gaspareau, on Baie Verte, at "exorbitant cost." See notes 31 and 32 for details on these forts. See page 90 for an illustration of the interior of Fort Beauséjour.**

have put himself in the place that he allowed to be taken by the English where their fort presently is. The advantage that the possession of their fort gives them over us is completely disadvantageous to us. If this officer had put himself where they are, the ships from Quebec which carry provisions to our garrisons would have entered the river as far as the foot of the fort as you have seen, which would as you well know spare the king transportation expenses for carting the provisions for the Beauséjour garrison over four leagues of road.[32] I agree that the generals cannot see everything, that they are obliged to rely on the commandants whom they appoint who often deceive them because they care only about their present interests [and] furthermore are often without knowledge [and] without foresight of what is appropriate to do for the advantage of the country [and] for the good of the service, which demonstrates that everything depends upon the choice of commandants, that officers who have never gone out or who are but newly in the service,[33] neither one or the other can have the experience and the knowledge that senior officers have who have NAC 2909 140v given proof of their wisdom, of their knowledge, and of their capacity, by the long industry they have devoted to the service. When one is busy only in obtaining furs, only in selling merchandise, only in making one's fortune at the king's expense, as these favored commandants are doing, one cannot keep informed about everything that can contribute to the greatest good of the service and to the knowledge of the regions where you [*sic*] are commanding and where you pass through. What wisdom, what knowledge can such officers give to a general who can inform the court only from the reports that are given to him, if he is given false ones, as has happened and is happening only too often? It is known all too well that the court is being deceived, but it is necessary to be silent. Since you tell me that the court is often obliged to close its eyes and to be silent itself in order not to be obliged to mete out punishment, I have nothing else to reply to you;** with the foregoing, all is said, and that is why I am going to speak to you about Michilimaquinac.

I have stated to you that it was the entrepôt of the northern posts. The commandants and traders of each post leaving Montreal stop at Michilimackinac in order to take on supplies, Indian corn or Turkish NAC 2910 corn[34] and bear's fat and even some of them canoes to continue on their way. These same commanders and traders go down from their posts every year to Michilimackinac, the commandants come to obtain their provisions and the general's orders, the merchants to bring their furs and to receive their trade goods. Several merchants from the Ylinois river and even some Jllinois [*sic*] come to sell their furs at this post for trade goods[35] 141r that they take back.

The Indians from all these posts, either to go down to Montreal or to take their furs to the English, pass through Michilimackinac in following the route linking it to Detroit through Lake Huron and Ste. Clere [Lake Saint Clair] whose discharge flows past Detroit and forms a river of around a half league in width which flows into Lake Herrier [Lake Erie]. This reveals the connection that all the northern nations have with those of the south and unfortunately with all the English with whom they have secret dealings, as well as the Indians from the southern part, one and the other via Lake Herrier and the Niagara portage which is three leagues long. [They] pass in front of the Niagara fort, where they trade some furs that the English do not take, for the goods they do not find at their place

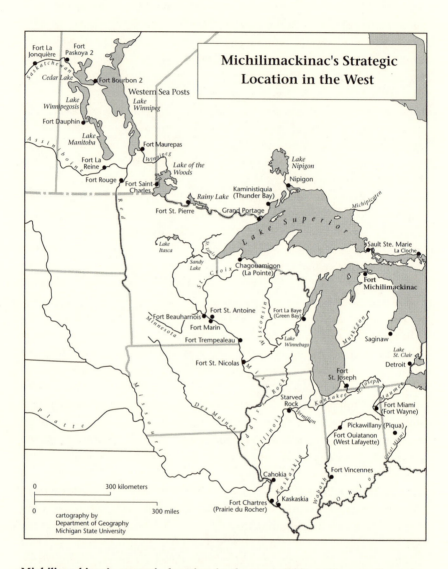

Michilimackinac's Strategic Location in the West

Michilimackinac's strategic location in the west. This major post "was the entrepôt of the northern posts (NAC 2909)." It supplied essential provisions for French military and trading posts as far away as the Western Sea posts in the northwest and served as a major trading post and fur-transshipment center. It also served importantly as a staging area for the French and their allied Indians in campaigns against the Iroquois, Foxes, Chickasaws, and Miamis.

and for provisions for going to Chouaguin [Chouaguen, Choueguen; Oswego, New York] and to Orange [Albany, New York] where they bring all their beaver and other good furs.[36] Besides the English taking away from us in Canada a trade that we would conduct which amounts to around *two million* [livres], and which many people would not be able to believe because that is not as known to them as it is to me, [since I] devoted myself in the various commands that were entrusted to me— NAC 2911 especially in the Niagara one which is the main key to Canada and the passage for all the nations of the country that go to the English, and in the command of the Miami post—to learning by serious study everything that could contribute the most to the greatest advantage of the king's service, to the retention of the country, and to the increase in our trade. If I 141v had not had the ambition to make myself capable of usefully serving the king, I would not have acquired the knowledge upon which I am drawing up this little report to satisfy the desire you have to know the interior of Canada and to know how the officer corps can be put into a decent, livable condition while considerably saving the king's annual expenses in all the posts without its costing anything to the public as I shall show you following this.

But why tell me, how is it of any use to you to go to this trouble, to make yourself so qualified from the knowledge you have acquired? Has the court rewarded you for it? Has it promoted your generals for you and have they shown any greater consideration for you? In the 32 years that you have been dedicating yourself to the service, have they granted you any posts which have made it possible for you to live decently?[37] It is true that neither the court nor the generals until now have given me any con- NAC 2912 sideration, that I am but a captain, that I have used up the assets that I had, and that there remains for me only 1,062 livres that I have as my [annual] pay and it costs me 1,600 livres to live at the inn. If I had not neglected up to the point of disdain my own self-interest in favor of the king's, I would at least have what I need to live on. If it is my misfortune that no one has any consideration for my disinterestedness, my zeal and my diligence, at least I have the honor of having served well and very faithfully my prince and my country. I am only more impoverished for it, it is true, however that does not discourage me.

Honor alone motivates me. I shall admit to you that often I am NAC 2913 depressed but what good does it do to distract myself and turn away from 142r my topic which I shall take up again in having you observe that besides this prodigious number of furs of which our Indians deprive us by taking

them to the English who profit from them and use this occasion to corrupt them and win them over, they make them into creatures at their
disposal to carry the spirit of revolt that they insinuate into them in all
their villages. We have experienced what I am saying in this latest war, by
the revolt of these same nations that killed many of our Frenchmen,
namely in the southern region, at Detroit, among the Miami, among the
8yatanon, at the Vermillon [River] in the Illinois country.[38]

In the northern region, in the Saginant [Saguinan; Saginaw,
Michigan], at La Cloche,[39] at the Chodière [Chaudière],[40] at La Baye, in
all of Lake Huron and at Michilimakinac; and this does not even include
the French who have been killed at Fort St. Frédéric or in the Montreal
district, like [those] at Isle Perault [Ile Perrot][41] and the Cèdres
[Cedars].[42]

I observe therefore that if there had been at Michilimakinac a sufficient garrison to impress the Indians of the northern posts, that [*sic*] they
NAC 2914   would not have dared kill any Frenchman. They did it because they saw
us there without troops or Frenchmen to resist them and repel their
aggression and to go help those various posts.[43] The Indians attack and
are brave only with the weak; where there is force to punish them, if
they do not [*sic*] fear it they remain quiet due to the fear they have of
142v   being killed when they see themselves as the weakest and even equal in
strength.

Whence I also observe that it is during peacetime that it is necessary
to put oneself in a state of being able to resist one's enemies, to repel
them and to make oneself feared by them. In order to succeed in this and
in the other worthy objectives it is appropriate, despite all that can be
said about it, to have at Michilimakinac a garrison as suitable as it should
be for the good of the service which would be a source of help and a
support for Detroit, just as the Detroit garrison would be for
Michilimakinac. With these two entrepôts well provided with troops, the
upper country nations would not dare move, especially if care were taken
to close and guard well the routes by which they go to the English. You
NAC 2915   have only three, especially two of interest. One can decide upon this last
course of action and cover them so well that nothing will be able to penetrate, nor force you to give way there; and no longer take anything
whatever into all the posts of the north and south; do not permit any
merchant to go there, nor any Frenchman; make all those who are there
come back. In that way you will subjugate all your Indians and you will
reduce them to the necessity of coming to throw themselves at your feet

to beg you with tears in their eyes not to abandon them. In that way you will compel them to come to you, to bring their furs in order to satisfy their ordinary needs which they will not be able to do without. From then on they will no longer lay down the law to the French, it will be you doing it to them and with the conditions that you want.

There are only the five Yrocois [Iroquois] nations,[44] because their villages are placed where they are, that you would not be able to prevent going to the English because they are between you and the English; but by guarding your three routes the Yrocois would not be able to bring help to your northern and southern nations. Furthermore you scarcely profit from the Yrocois trade. In losing them, you would benefit from it. If this decision were made they would be wild wanting to be entirely on the side of the French. If this last decision were made, you would no longer need any commandant in all the posts of the north, nor among the Miami and 8ÿatanon. It is necessary to keep the one at Detroit with respect to the French who are settled there, but do not let any merchandise be brought there for the use of the Indians, especially guns, powder, lead, axes, and kettles. You will no longer have any other posts to occupy but Fort Frontenac and your three passages.

But it must be noted that the Petit Rapide [Buffalo, New York] which is at the entrance to Lake Herrier is the principal and most important [of the three passages] because you defend this passage within musket range, and that at Fort Niagara you cannot prevent any canoe from passing, the river being very nearly a quarter of a league wide.[45] If all this were followed, all your Indian nations would be reduced to the necessity of coming to trade at Montreal. From then on you would completely be their masters, the routes for going to the English being closed. If we had Chöaguin [Oswego] blown up and if you were able to maintain yourselves there, you would have but two passages to guard to prevent the Indians from going to Orange and to Filadelfil. Rarely would they take this route because of the long march that they would have to make by land. It would also be necessary to observe that in the Ylinois country absolutely no merchandise is provided them for their use. All the Indians not being able to go any longer to the English would surely get tired of coming from so far to Montreal in order to obtain their necessities. If anyone[46] suggested to them that normally we would bring them their necessities only on one condition, which would be for them, by themselves, to chase the English out of Chöaguin and the Belle Rivière if there continue [*sic*] to be any there and for them to forbid their ever

143r

NAC 2916

143v

NAC 2917

appearing there again and that if they were to come back it would cost them their lives, I dare guarantee that every nation would accept it.[47]

If you conclude that you should not make that decision, and that it is more advantageous to leave things as they presently are, you have not thought of the considerable savings that you would make regarding the great number of habitants who leave your fields to take the great number of canoes that go annually into all parts of the north and south to trade among the Indian nations, who would henceforth spend their time only in clearing and cultivating your land instead of spending it as they do only on these kinds of trips, [you have not thought of] the great increase in the settlement and in the productivity of your land, of the considerable savings of the expenses of this trade that you would conduct as well without leaving where you live. If all these advantages do not win acceptance, you, in insisting on continuing the present system, would not be **144r** able then to deny the necessity of a town at Detroit, and of a headquar-**NAC 2918** ters, a garrison at Michilimakinac as I said under the orders of a major in command. As for the garrison's supplies, I have the easiest means for its subsistence and an arrangement known to me that would spare the king many expenditures besides all transport costs if one considered granting me this command and what would be suitable to accelerate my project.

I have just spoken to you about the way to remove the opportunity for our Indians to go to the English at Chöaguin by closing the routes by which they go there. The commandant who replaced me in the Niagara command when I received orders from Monsieur de La Galisonnière[48] [*sic*] to go take command of the post of the Miami who had revolted before and who were conspiring against us with the other nations in revolt and calling the English, believed he had found the way to remove from our Indians the opportunity to go to the English at Choaguin and at Orange. Without having examined his idea very much, he sent it in. It was supported by Sieur Varin, commissary at Montreal,[49] his brother-in-law, who as a result obtained orders for building, as was done, at the end [head] of the Niagara portage at about one-third of a league or more dis-**NAC 2919** tant from the trail on the left, a wooden fort, lodgings, a storehouse for conducting the brandy trade that is done there.[50] It was believed that this attraction, which was shifted from the Niagara fort, where it was sold before, to this new fort would stop the Indians all the more effectively since they would spare themselves the trouble of taking the portage **144v** which is three leagues long as I believe I have already said, which however did not happen as it had been imagined. In fact it was only a poorly

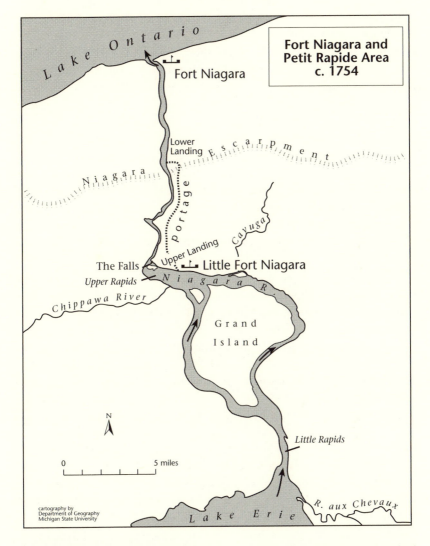

The Fort Niagara and Petit Rapide area, ca. 1754. By 1758 the French had established a post at the Petit Rapide, only to have it fall to the British with Fort Niagara the following year.

thought-out dream. They only go all the more to the English because of it. If they had had the least bit of experience and had thought it out sensibly, they would have known that effort costs the Indians nothing, and having gone into the portage it costs them nothing more to continue as they are doing. Of what use then is this [wooden] fort?[51] It serves those whom the king pays and feeds and maintains there to do the trading that it is said his majesty has ordered to be done for his account and profit; to do it [trading] by having them [those trading for the king] send to Montreal by means of the voyageurs who bring down to Montreal from Detroit the furs that they [the voyageurs] trade there [at Detroit]; and the beaver that they [the king's traders at the wooden fort] trade, they have it taken to Chöaguin by Indians who are totally devoted to them for which they have English cloth, printed calico, and other prohibited goods brought in that they [the king's traders] sell to these same voyageurs when they go back up to Detroit. I know it because I have seen it; I

NAC 2920 know it as well because those voyageurs who did not hide from me told me so.

If this fort had been placed at the Petit Rapide of which I have spoken it would have produced marvels and the expected effect. I had proposed it to Monsieur le marquis de la Galissonnière [*sic*] when I was in command at Niagara. This general filled with wisdom and knowledge had recognized its necessity and advantages and had given orders to establish this fort at the Petit Rapide. Monsieur de La Jonquière who replaced him, who did not have the same perspicacity, allowed himself to

145r   be deceived and won over.

II

In speaking to you about the Petit Rapide I did not have you take note that I pointed out to you the route that Michilimackinac and all the northern nations have through Lakes Huron and Ste. Clere with Detroit and Lake Herrier which is their discharge and also the trails to the Belle Rivière posts. I told you that almost all the nations of the northern and southern parts go to the English only via Lake Herrier. Well, observe that the Petit Rapide closes this lake; that its passage is so

NAC 2921 narrow that from one bank to the other a man could be killed by musket;[52] that it is the only passage navigable by canoe; and that the other passage has a portage of more than twenty leagues—it is Toronteaux; that being well established at Petit Rapide you block all the northern and

Aerial view of Fort Niagara, ca. 1990. *OFN (dup) 7701/12. Courtesy Old Fort Niagara.*

southern nations; that you have a firm support base and a solid and sure entrepôt for your posts at the Belle Rivière, Detroit, the Miami and 8yatanon; that from the Niagara portage and the Chenondac River [Chippewa Creek, Welland River[53]], you can create superb settlements, as we have other more critical locations.

Let us observe that if you occupy the Petit Rapide only on the occasion of the first war that we shall have with the English, it is to be feared that the five Yrocois nations and their allies who are all at their disposition will declare war on us. In this case they will not fail to seize the Petit Rapide, call the English, and establish them there. It is easy for them to go there via the Nontaguay [Onontagué; Onondaga] and the Sonontouin [Sonontouan, Tsonnontouan; Seneca] without your being able to oppose it. If that occurs as it would not fail to, you will instantly lose Niagara. It will not be possible for you to hold on to it. Even less 145v will you go to all your posts that are in the southern part since by losing NAC 2922 the Petit Rapide you lose the route to them. Even if you were able to keep Niagara, I suppose, you would not retake the Petit Rapide. You would be crushed, cut to pieces before getting there even were you to attack it in the winter. With difficulty you would hold on to Fort Frontenac. Toronteaux would be defeated and burned. If the enemy occupied it, would you pass easily through the north in order to retake Niagara or the Petit Rapide?

You will open a route for yourself via Choaguin which you will be able to take, I expect. Are you sure you can keep it? I admit that it would be most advantageous and worthwhile to take Chouaguin and to be able to keep it. It is Chouaguin that attracts all our Indians and which has corrupted them all. The greatest error that General de Beauharnois made was to have suffered the English to build that settlement that he was free to prevent. The occasion of the hit-and-run warfare[54] of the Belle Rivière could presently be used or the next break between France and England to chase the English from it, but first it is necessary to examine with great deliberation whether it is more advantageous to take Choaguin than to go to war with the Five Nations. As it is they who NAC 2923 gave them this territory and guaranteed its possession to them, they will attack us. If we have war with the Five Nations and their allies, how will you keep, as I have already said, Niagara, the Petit Rapide which is the 146r passage to all the southern posts? How will you escort your convoys to bring them help? How will you supply all your detachments and war parties? You have no troops, you do not even presently have any to provide the least needs of the present service which is indispensable. Will you continue, as you are doing, to strip your fields of your habitants? If you continue to do so, as you will be obliged to, your land will remain uncultivated. You are taking life away from your people, from yourself; you are decreasing all your support in provisions that to the contrary you must find a way to increase for this occasion, to be able to resist your enemies and repulse them.

You have seen the advantage of the establishment of the Petit Rapide. Here is another outcome from that advantage. As the fort would be accessible to the French who trade at Detroit, among the Miami, among the 8ÿatanon, and Ilinois, [and] who come to sell their furs at Montreal—when they do not sell them at Detroit to spare themselves 170 leagues of travel, the portage costs, the food costs, and wages for NAC 2924 *engagés*[55] to man their canoes, [and] the expense for their wintering at Montreal—[these French traders] would prefer, in order to spare themselves all these costs, to sell their furs at the king's storehouse at the Petit Rapide for the goods they need for the fur trade. The Indian nations of which we have spoken would also do their trading there in order to spare themselves the long distance they would have to cover to go to Choagain [*sic*], which is more than 90 leagues away, and in order to return sooner to their villages, including the most distant, before the winter.   **146v**

The king in order to spare himself the expense of transporting supplies proportionately to the garrisons of the forts of the Belle Rivière, Detroit, Michilimackinac if garrisons are placed there, can place at the Petit Rapide one or two barks,[56] which will be loaded for their return with furs from the traders of these posts that they would unload [from their canoes] at the Petit Rapide, where the freightage would be paid in furs at the price of the place, which would reimburse the expenses and upkeep of the barks. Well beyond, bateaux[57] would bring them [the furs] to Fort Niagara where the barks from Fort Frontenac would take them. The *batteaux du cent*[58] that bring provisions there would take them down [from Fort Frontenac] to Montreal where the last three legs of the trip would also be paid in furs, which would be a profit for the king and a very considerable savings for the merchants, for the canoes, wages, and food for the *engagés* they would need for transporting their furs.[59] Before   NAC 2925
constructing these barks, it would be necessary to examine the locations where they could drop anchor and take shelter from the wind if they were surprised or impeded by it. If barks are not desired you would need greater canoe and transport expenditures.

You have therefore seen and had to notice that with the Petit Rapide settled and well guarded, the Indians can no longer go to Chöagain; it follows that its trade will fall off, and in falling off it is no longer of any use whatever to the English; they built it only to take away   **147r**
our trade with our nations. If we ever came to being at war with the Indians, Chöagain would be very dangerous for us because it would provide a retreat for them. No matter how, it is necessary to take Chöagain or put ourselves in a situation whereby it will not be able to harm us. Observe however that the English are cutting into us through the two ends of Canada. They began by establishing Choagain on Lake Hontario [Ontario] to the east-southeast of this lake at a distance of 25 leagues from Fort Frontenac and around 70 from Niagara, and from the same direction they can go to these two forts in barks and in boats just as we can go to them. They can go down to Montreal in boats and come in barks as far as La Galette [Ogdensburg, New York], which is 35 leagues distant from Montreal.

They have gone subsequently to the Belle Rivière, through which   NAC 2926
they can go to Detroit, to the Miami, to the 8ÿatanon, to the Ilinois.

They are trading via the Belle Rivière and at the Belle Rivière itself with all the nations. They can come to Niagara (never if the Petit Rapide is settled and made capable of defending itself). They have established themselves at the foot of the River at Chibouctou [Halifax, Nova Scotia]; at La Baye Verte, within sight of our Beauséjour garrison; last year in the spring at Mirligaiche [Mirliguèche; Lunenburg, Nova Scotia] where they threw in eighteen hundred families all at once.[60] These last three settlements block the River of Canada [St. Lawrence River]. If they settle the Gaspé as they say they will, if that happens, we will be obliged to surrender to them without their being obliged to fire a musket

147v   shot. They will be but one hundred leagues from Quebec. No vessel however big or small it might be will be able to go there. From that time on there is no further help from France to hope for.

Last spring the Abenaki reported that they [the English] established a fort below Naransonac [Naransouack; Norridgewock, Maine?]. The first Abenaki who had come from that direction had said that they had built a fort in the village of Naransonac itself and another on the

NAC 2927   Naransonac River [Kennebec River] 4 leagues above and that they had gone up this river [Kennebec] as far as the source of the Pentagouet River [Penobscot River, Maine] which is the height of the land [Mount Kineo, Maine?] where there is a lake [Moosehead Lake, Maine] and a portage of 4 leagues [Northeast Carry?] where the separation occurs of the waters that go down to the sea by the Naransonac [Kennebec] River, and on our side they [the waters] go down by Sasagues8enaudin into Lake Namekantic [Lac Mégantic; Lake Megantic, Province of Quebec] which flows into the Saut de la Chaudière River [the falls of the Chaudière River, P.Q.].[61] These Abenaki had said that the English had built a third fort on Lake Namekantic where the Sasagues8enadin River flows into this lake. This location is only 35 leagues from our habitants of Nouvelle Bosse [Beauce][62] and only 45 to 50 from Quebec. Indians were sent to find out if this report is true. All of that shows the designs the English have to take Canada away from us since they are putting themselves into position to attack us everywhere, as they can do at the onset of war. The panic fear that they have of the Indians must bring us to employ everything to keep all our Indian nations faithful which would be of very great use upon that occasion when it would be neces-sary not to fail to besiege Baston [Boston] by sea and by land by moving

148r   down to keep their maritime forces busy in that direction in order to permit our ships to go into Canada and to create a diversion for the

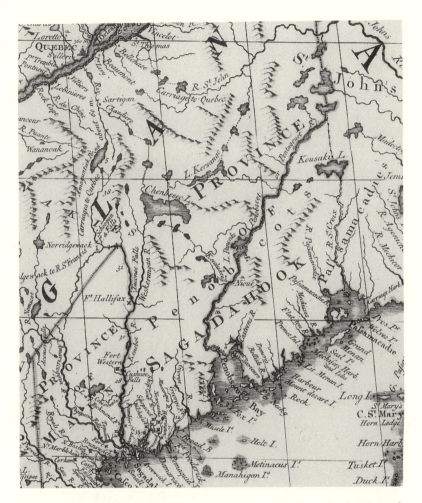

1755 map showing potential invasion routes to Quebec via the Kennebec River or Penobscot River and the Chaudière River, all mentioned by Raymond. This British map by John Mitchell shows Fort Western (Augusta, Maine), Fort Halifax (Winslow, Maine), Norridgewock (Naransonac in Raymond's *dénombrement*), the Kennebec River leading to "Chenbesec Lake" (Moosehead Lake) "at the height of the land," near the "separation of the waters" (between Moosehead Lake and the western branch of the Penobscot River). The Moose River actually flows on an east–west axis linking Moosehead Lake to a portage to the Chaudière River and is not accurately depicted. *Detail from Map of the British and French Dominions in North America . . . by John Mitchell, 1755. Reproduced with permission of the William L. Clements Library, University of Michigan.*

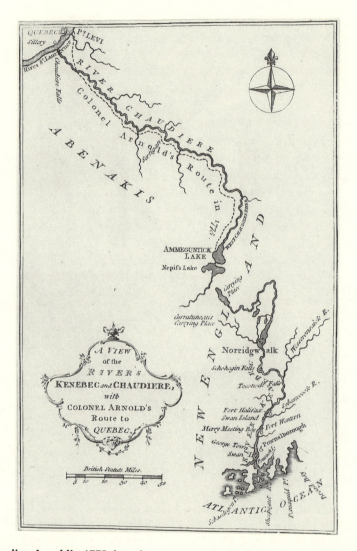

Benedict Arnold's 1775 invasion route early in the American Revolution. Arnold proceeded north on the Kennebec through Fort Western, Fort Halifax, Norridgewock, and the Great Carrying Place (between the Kennebec and Dead rivers) to the Chaudière River and Quebec. *"A View of the Rivers Kennebec and Chaudière, with Colonel Arnold's Route to Quebec" (ZAN-591), London Magazine, September 1776, map reproduced by permission of the Map Division of the New York Public Library, Astor and Tilden Foundations.* Arnold's remarkable invasion and siege of Quebec, while failing at Quebec, confirm Raymond's concern with this area.

troops that they designated to take it, that they would be obliged to keep NAC 2928
busy to defend Baston and Port Royal [Annapolis Royal, Nova Scotia]. I
see no other way to save this colony if the English attack it. And to
remove the possibility of establishing themselves at Naransonac and on
this side of it, and along the Belle Rivière to have them continually
harassed by our allied Indians, pay them 40# or 50# apiece for as many
English scalps as they bring. I answer you that they will soon abandon
their settlements and leave our lands peaceful without putting you to the
trouble of leaving your home. What is more, one defeats one's enemies
as one can and I believe that that is permitted as soon as it is a question
of preserving the state and one's country.[63]

After having enumerated the Canadian posts of the upper country
for you, having shown you their positions and the routes linking them,
and having given you an idea of the region and spoken about the nature
of the Indians and the way to lead them, let us proceed with the rest. ★**I**
have told you that it was definitely not rank or seniority which, since I
have been in Canada and until now, have determined the choice of officers to command at these posts; that it was through favoritism, and NAC 2929
almost always to the same individuals and to the same families, that the
rich posts have been given. They no longer leave the hands of the families named Ramezai [Ramezay], La Corne, Marin father and son, (the
father was the son of a sergeant of the troops), de Repentigni
[Repentigny], Villiers, Beaujeu, Dumuis [De Muy], Celoron, Laperrière
[La Perrière], Péan, and Mercier who presently have the whole Ilinois
River. The first has La Pointe with St. Luc La Corne [La Corne St. Luc]
and half of many other posts.[64] Many other French families and officers 148v
are deprived of them although they have given on several occasions satis-
factory proof of their knowledge, their dedication, and their zeal and disinterestedness, officers who devote themselves only to the good of the
service and who, however, have never been granted any of these commands which would have put them in a position to maintain their service, who remain destitute and cannot provide enough for their families
to live on. The French and Canadian officers who are not married: is
their salary as captain which is but 1,062# sufficient to pay 1,200# for
room and board without a servant, and 1,600# with a servant?[65] It is
generally known that they [room and board] are on that basis. Where can
they obtain the difference to pay it or obtain their keep when they have
no other resource but such a feeble salary in a country where the cost of
everything and even of life itself is prohibitive? What must we do then to

NAC 2930

remain alive and have clothing? That is the least that can be granted to the lowest of men. However, persons of quality, senior and good officers, do not have it. In order to have it, must they steal? No. What then is to be done in this dire need? We borrow from merchants almost all of whom lose what they have loaned to officers who die insolvent, which would never happen if instead of giving everything through favoritism, or instead of appropriating everything in concert with their favorites they were careful to assign officers to these commands each in turn, and unfortunately it is not done. What is the result? That all the officers

149r

who are deprived of the help from these posts are scorned by those who are in favor, even by the soldier and the people. From this an unbelievable insubordination follows. The nouveau riche, favored subaltern scarcely acknowledges acquaintance with a senior captain who has turned gray under the weight of his arms; even less does he show him due respect. Once again, what is the result? A distaste for the service, no more diligence, no more zeal, no more concern for the king. That is the fruit produced by the discontent in the officers who are neglected, rejected, and left destitute despite their urgent entreaties to be put to good use.

NAC 2931

Those who are in favor are profiting from the times, are occupied only in earning money, are neglecting their most essential duties, are in no way working for the good of the service. Their lack of experience and their ignorance make them incapable of turning in any reports. Their being in favor and their money take the place of knowledge, for most of them have been and are obliged to use the voyageurs' hand in order to fulfill this duty.

That is how, by both sides, the king is poorly served, [by] the former due to discontent, [by] the latter due to incompetence. How can such a great evil be remedied, and what means can be employed to restore the soul of the service, to draw emulation out of torpor, to renew application and awaken the ambition to become competent and be interested only in the good of the service and the means of achieving it in order to serve usefully?

149v

This means is to have the individuals who are placed in office to govern this country extend their favor among all the officers. Let there be no further unjust preference; let these commands, as you have seen the results of them, be granted only to the captains; let the subalterns be placed under their orders as second-in-command; let them be given on the basis of seniority, experience, and attention of the officers to their

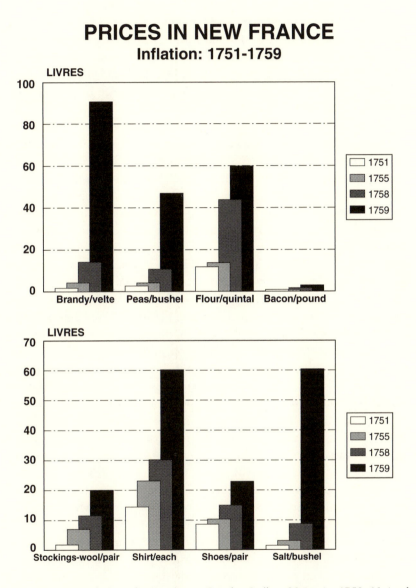

PRICES IN NEW FRANCE
Inflation: 1751-1759

Source: Exposition du Prix des Denrées en Canada, Québec, 20 janvier 1759, National Archives of Canada: MG 5, B1: Ministère des Affaires étrangères (Paris), Mémoires et Documents: Amérique, 11:85-90 (transcripts of folios 72v-73v). Graph by Jack Saylor.★

★For the translated complete list of commodity prices in these years, see Peyser, *Jacques Legardeur de Saint-Pierre*, 239.

NAC 2932   duties; let a fund be created from the income of all the posts in general from which the supplementary pay[66] will be taken by a fair arrangement for allocation to all the captains and subalterns employed in these posts. From this fund take the supplementary pay, and wages of the chaplains, storekeepers, surgeons, bakers, blacksmiths, wagoners, the expense of cutting the hay, wood, chimney sweeping, maintenance of the forts, and other expenses. These last items are only for the forts where the king keeps garrisons. The start of this project should all at once focus on the large annual expenditures spared his majesty which will no longer leave his coffers and which remove from all rogues the means for robbing the king with impunity. All those who did not have shoes on their feet four or five years ago who are today millionaires who are having palaces built, who have several seagoing vessels, who for considerable sums send for silverware from France, who have land bought for them for one hundred thousand *écus* and four hundred thousand francs,[67] would not approve this

150r   plan. They would destroy it and would bring to bear a thousand ways to prevent its execution if it were known and sufficiently appreciated to be approved and its orders given. The posts of La Baye, la Mer du Ouest

NAC 2933   [*sic*], La Pointe, Detroit, and many others; the interior and exterior trade of this colony, the furnishing of baked goods and meat, and the expenditure of several million [livres] which appear to have been used up for two thousand men who were made to march last year to construct out of wood Fort Presqu'isle, the one at Rivière au boeuf, and this year the one named Fort Duquesne;[68] for the construction of which—and the detachment of M. de Villiers who was going to avenge the death of his brother—they had around 1,500 men march. That is what makes such quick fortunes. But tell me, the accommodating attitude I have in telling you so many truths, to let you know Canada well, will have me banished, I am afraid. Well, let us then say no more other than to tell you that as for the commanders who have no garrisons and who are not on the route of the annual journey up and down of all the officers and traders of the other posts, as they are not subject to any expense, it would be necessary to leave them to the thousand écus of supplementary pay that they are given when the trade of the post that they command has not been given to them. This supplementary pay is reasonable, as they have no other expenditures to make but for themselves.★★

NAC 2934   **As for the commandants** whose duty brings about many expendi-
150v   tures it would be necessary to give them proportional supplementary pay and bring their supplies free to one and the other as that is the practice

which the traders of each post are obliged to follow. We shall now examine all these various details.

The commandants of Forts Frontenac and Niagara are subject to two inevitable and indispensable expenditures, the first for the officers, cadets, chaplains and storekeeper of their garrisons, the second expenditure for the detachments of officers and cadets and the heads of trading expeditions who go up to and come down from the various posts which are above them in the southern region.

The one at Detroit [has expenses] for the garrison's officers, those who go up and come down from the Miami and 8ÿatanon, the missionaries, and traders at his post.

The one at Michilimakinac [has expenses] for the officers, missionaries, and traders at his post, for the officers who go up and those from all the northern posts who come down from them every year, as I said, and spend a certain amount of time there, which brings about a very great expenditure. In consideration of this these four commandants[69] should be given supplementary pay proportional to this expense and to their con- NAC 2935 siderable work since they are on the route to and provide the entrepôts for the other posts and the access and route to all the nations. That is what gives them many time-consuming occupations and that is what also creates the need in these four posts for levelheaded, wise, cautious, perspicacious, and very experienced captains who like the work and who are able to report well and reliably.   151r

Fort St. Frederic not being on the route to any post, the commandant is subject to no expense but that of the officers of the garrison if he is honorable. That is why his supplementary pay will be one thousand écus like that of the officers who have no expenditure to make. The subalterns, the chaplain, the surgeon, and other employees will ordinarily be given ordinary rations. Fort St. Jean [on the Richelieu River] will be treated in the same way.

Saut [Sault] Ste. Marie has been granted as a seigniory both to Sieur de Bonne and his own [people] with exclusive trading rights; for this reason there is no supplementary pay to be attached to this post. Sr. de Bonne, being its seigneur and commandant, receives more than supplementary pay from the big income from this post and that is being well treated indeed for a new arrival in a country without having performed any service there. Officers who have 30 and 40 years of service who have NAC 2936 performed remarkably would be quite happy to be treated like him, I first after 32 years of continuous, consistent, and assiduous service which has been praised by the minister as you know from everything he wrote about me to the general of this country who is completely indifferent about it, however.[70]

In order to create the fund about which I have spoken to you it would be necessary to place all the posts on a congé basis, with the congés set at one hundred pistoles,[71] as they were in the past, even in the time of General Beauharnois, at Detroit and Michilimakinac, and whose 151v price was reduced only since the last war in consideration of the risks run by the merchants who do business in these posts.

If these congés were to have different prices it would only be those at the lowest price which would be filled out.[72] The others would only be sold with difficulty. One must expect as I have said that this memoir would have many enemies if orders were given to carry it out. The self-same merchants would make difficulties appear in order to obtain these congés for less than one hundred pistoles and to have the number of them decrease. One has but to respond that if they do not purchase the number of congés at the established price, they will not be forced to do so; that the king will farm out all these posts to his account and profit; NAC 2937 that if they allow this decision to be made, they will no longer be welcome to have the posts to continue the upper country trade. This language will astonish them so much that all of them being indebted to this trade for their prosperity and being able to keep it and procure it for themselves only by this means which I might add is the outlet for their merchandise, they will prefer to fill out the congés and pay one hundred pistoles for them, rather than not be able to continue a trade to which they owe their well-being.

But to make things easier for the merchants they can be permitted to form partnerships with several together in order to obtain the congés for each post and to continue them for as long as they wish or at least for six years.

As for those merchants who will purchase the congés for Forts Frontenac, Toronteaux, Niagara including the Petit Rapide if it were to 152r be established, being inseparable from Niagara, to facilitate transporting their goods, let the king furnish them with *batteaux du cent* and not the tackle, which they will maintain and replace if they lose any in going up to or coming down from the above forts. The king will also provide them with the barks and only the tackle with which they are fitted upon taking them, and when they return them they will return them with the NAC 2938 tackle in the same condition and in the same quantity, both barks and

Congé issued by La Jonquière on 29 May 1750 to St. Dizier, a merchant, to take one canoe with six men and trade goods for trading at Michilimackinac only, on condition of taking along 500 pounds of the king's supplies for the post. The names and addresses of Dizier's six *engagés* are listed at the bottom of the congé. *Reproduced with permission of the Archives nationales du Québec, Direction de l'Ouest du Québec, Congés de traite TL4, S34, 29 mai 1750.*

tackle, that one and the other were when they were given to them. If they happen to lose some barks they will be lost on their own accounts; they will have them replaced at their own expense. When the boats and barks are worn out through aging the king will have them replaced at his expense because one and the other would have been equally worn out if His Majesty had continued to exploit the above-mentioned posts on his own account as he is doing.

In consideration of the advantage that the king would give them by providing them with his batteaux and barks, they will deliver and bring back the troops being stationed in the aforementioned posts and their equipment and clothing; they will also take and bring back the workers whom it will be necessary to send when there are repairs to be made. And to avoid the considerable expense of transporting the provisions for these garrisons and the goods that the king trades there, it will be suitable for the merchants who purchase the congés for Forts Frontenac, Toronteaux, Niagara, and Petit Rapide, if it were to be established, to provide the provisions to the garrisons of these posts, that is to say to the soldiers only, to the barber, surgeon, to the workers for the repairs when they are needed and those [provisions] which the commandants are in the course of their duty obliged to give to the Indians, to the couriers passing through or detached from the posts. It would be necessary to determine the price of this supplying at so much per hundredweight of bread and bacon,[73] and at so much per hundredweight of tobacco, lead, powder; at so much per bushel of peas, in the event that the king were obliged to take some for presents to the Indians. So many soldiers' rations of bread and bacon make so many hundredweight; so many habitants' rations of bread and bacon make so many hundredweight; so many *pots*[74] of brandy make so many *veltes*,[75] and at so much per *velte*. Let this supplying be done by putting it out to bid, taking the average of the highest price and the lowest price at which wheat is valued, and pigs and the other foods according to the most or the least that the harvests and the country provide. Let the price from this bidding be set for good, since its price would be set by taking the mean of the highest and lowest prices. Supposing that cereals, pork, and other foodstuffs now become dear and now inexpensive, as that happens, the balance will be equal between the king and the most or the least expensive suppliers. Bread will be made from pure wheat and flour only refined for bran alone. Inspection of provisions of bread and bacon that are spoiled and of poor quality will be carried out by the commandants, officers, and chaplains

152v

NAC 2939

of the garrisons in the presence of the suppliers. When they have been NAC 2940
judged and condemned as such, the loss will be borne by the suppliers,
who will be obliged and constrained to provide some of a good and 153r
healthful quality and to send away the bad in order to avoid sicknesses
and the desertion of the soldiers from dissatisfaction, all the more so
since five livres a month are withheld from a soldier's pay for the food
that the king provides to him.

As for the commandants, junior officers, and chaplains of these forts,
the king will no longer provide them with food or any gear. They will
provide them to themselves by means of the supplementary pay which
will be paid to them. They [their provisions] will only be brought to
them at their posts gratis by the merchants who obtain the congés of
these posts as is practiced elsewhere.

By this arrangement the king saves the provisions and wages of the
storekeepers, of clerks that are brought to them; the provisions for their
families, who are useless and a burden to the king; the provisions and
wages of the bakers, blacksmiths; the provisions for their families, who
provide no service to His Majesty; the supplies and wages of the interpreters—the merchants will be obliged to use them when the commandants have to speak to the Indians—the food and the wages of the
carters; the horses' feed; and the upkeep of the harnesses and carts will NAC 2941
be a shared expense regarding the firewood—for the officers, soldiers,
chaplains, barber surgeons—that it is necessary to cart from the places
where it is cut to the forts; the food and wages of a large number of
voyageurs who are occupied for seven months only in bringing in the
food and provisions of these garrisons; and the great quantity of goods 153v
for the trade that is carried out there with the Indians that is said to be to
the king's profit as it should be, the expenditure for it being at his
expense. He would also be spared a great quantity of bacon that is found
to be spoiled, stinking, because of the poor quality of the salting. This
loss amounts to more than six thousand livres. Those who are to see to
its good quality are those who supply it. That is done under an assumed
name in order to earn more. They have it prepared cut-rate with no care
at all and often have it purchased from private parties who, in order not
to be inspected, sell it to them at a good price. When I was second-in-
command at Fort Frontenac we sent back every year 15, 20, and 30
quarts[76] of bacon. When I commanded Niagara, every year I was obliged
to send back 20, 30, and 40 *quarts*, yet I used to pass on a great deal to
the Indians in order for the king to lose less. NAC 2942

Two-wheeled eighteenth-century Canadian *charrette* being drawn by three horses. The large number of horses here was dictated by the weight of the load and the hill. Detail from an engraving by J. Fougeron after a drawing by Richard Short published in 1761 and titled "A View of the Bishop's House. . ." [Quebec]. *Reproduced with the permission of the National Archives of Canada, C-352.*

One will, following this, see the savings about which I have spoken and those about which I have not yet said anything.

Determination of the actual numbers that the garrisons of Forts La Présentation, Frontenac, Toronteaux, and Niagara will have:

At Fort La Présentation in peacetime, it is pointless to have a commandant and a garrison . It is an expense which serves no purpose and which would be better used to establish the Petit Rapide, or for the expense of new settlements on the Belle Rivière. The merchants who would be placed there would be sufficient. Suppose that some [troops] would be wanted to continue there; let us calculate on that basis.

154r

At La Présentation

1 lieutenant as commandant

1 second ensign

10 soldiers. Since there is a missionary who is Abbé Piquet[77] and who has other priests with him, no chaplain will be necessary, nor a

surgeon since it is at the gates of Montreal. In 24 hours you are down there.

If the merchants who exploit the posts provide the food to the garrisons, through the bidding process of which we have already spoken, the king will no longer need, at La Présentation, at Fort Frontenac, at NAC 2943 Toronteaux, at Niagara, or in any garrison of the Belle Rivière and Detroit, any storekeeper, clerk, baker, blacksmiths. Forge work being part and parcel of the trade, it will be the merchants' responsibility. Carters, horses, their food and upkeep will be shared expenses as I have said. The merchants will not be able to do without them. Thus it is for all these garrisons and that is why I shall no longer repeat it.

At Fort Frontenac

1 captain as commandant
1 lieutenant
1 ensign
1 second ensign
1 chaplain
1 surgeon
30 soldiers including a sergeant and corporals
1 carter   **154v**
1 cowherd for the cows that are the king's

Out of the thirty soldiers of the garrison will be taken the lieutenant and 10 soldiers who will stay at Toronteaux from the first days of May until St. Michael's Day [29 September] to protect the merchants who are there during their trading. Once this is finished, the lieutenant and the ten soldiers will come back to Fort Frontenac. This will be the practice successively. In wartime the same number of officers and 50 soldiers of whom 20 will be sent to Toronteaux as stated above.

At Niagara

NAC 2944

1 captain
1 lieutenant
1 ensign
1 second ensign
1 chaplain
1 surgeon
40 soldiers all included

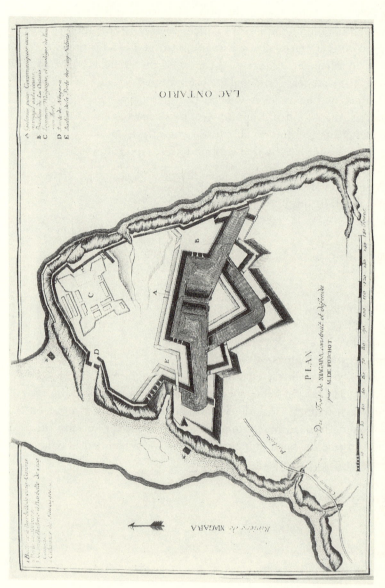

Plan of Fort Niagara, ca. 1756, by Pierre Pouchot, *Mémoires sur la dernière guerre de l'Amérique septentrionale entre la France et l'Angleterre. Suivis d'Observations, dont plusieurs sont relatives au théâtre actuel de la guerre, & de nouveaux détails sur les moeurs & les usages des Sauvages, avec des cartes topographiques,* 3 vols. (Yverdon, Switzerland, 1781), 1:182. *Courtesy William L. Clements Library, University of Michigan.*

1 carter

1 cowherd

If the merchants remain in the portage the lieutenant and 15 soldiers will be detached and will remain there to protect them during their trading from the first days of May until St. Michael's Day when they will return to the fort. If the merchants remain at Niagara only, the garrison will be made up of only 30 soldiers. If the Petit Rapide were established, it is there that it would be necessary to keep the garrison, which would be composed of the same number of officers as at Niagara and of 60 soldiers of whom 15 and the lieutenant would be detached to remain at Niagara. In wartime a captain, the same number of officers as at present, and 60 **155r** soldiers would be necessary there, and at the Petit Rapide 100 soldiers, 4 sergeants, 8 corporals, 2 drummers, a lieutenant, a full ensign, and a second ensign in addition.[78] 12 pieces of 8-pounder cannon would not be too much.

I said that the king would no longer provide any food or any gear to **NAC 2945** any officers, commandants, and junior officers, of any garrison or any post.

In order to eliminate jealousy and make it possible for the king to be better and more faithfully served, it is appropriate for the salary of all the commandants and all the officers on active duty, in all garrisons and all posts in general, to be equal. The difficulty and the duty being equal it is only the commandants of the four posts who I said must be paid more than the others in relation to the substantial expenses brought about by the assignment and passing through of officers and their garrisons [to other posts]. There is however no other way to prevent them from taking more of an interest in trading with the Indians than taking an interest in the good of the service. For, tell me, are there equality and justice in the annual salary of the upper country commandants? Some are given one thousand écus [3,000 livres] and others six hundred livres with 2 pounds of bread daily, 1/2 pound of bacon and a *barrique* [large barrel] of wine each year. Is this worth the 2,400 livres more that the former have? It is appropriate therefore for all the reasons that I have just shown you to cut out the miserable scraps of food and set all the supplementary pay at one **155v** thousand écus, and since they will provide their own food and it will be **NAC 2946** brought to them gratis, as it is done for those who are given one thousand écus, it is suitable to settle its transport according to the expense that they are obliged to incur.

Daily life in a French frontier fort (Fort Beauséjour in Acadia, ca. 1753; see Part III, notes 31 and 32). In 1754 most of the upper country forts were made of wood rather than stone, with garrisons of fewer than 30 *Troupes de la Marine.* **Noteworthy exceptions were Niagara and Fort de Chartres in the Illinois country.** *Detail from a painting by Lewis Parker titled "Fort Beauséjour during the French Régime," [Fort Beauséjour National Historic Site], reproduced with permission of the artist; photograph courtesy of Parks Canada.*

Regulation of the weight which will be carried to the commandants and junior officers on duty in the upper country posts, in order for them to live there, by the merchants who will be exploiting the posts:

To wit for each year

To the commandants of Fort Frontenac, Niagara, Detroit, Michilimakinac, to each 4,000 pounds weight;[79] for each junior officer serving under their orders, to the chaplains or missionaries, to each 1,800; to the surgeons of Detroit and Michilimakinac, to each 1,200.

To each of the captains commanding the posts of La Baye, St. Joseph, La Mer du Ouest, Kamanistigouÿa (Chaouamigon or La Pointe), Nepigon, La Belle Rivière, the Miami, 8ÿatanon, to the captains who will be in garrisons at Detroit [and] at Michilimakinac if they are placed there, 3,000.

To each of their seconds-in-command and officers of the aforesaid companies, 1,800; the same weight will be brought to the chaplains if they are placed in the Belle Rivière; and 1,200 to the surgeon at Fort Duquesne.

The soldiers of the garrisons of Detroit, Belle Rivière, the Miami, and NAC 2947 8ÿatanon, if the needs of the service require their being placed in these two last posts, if one wanted to feed these garrisons at less cost it is necessary to feed them with the same food that all the voyageurs live on, that is 156r Indian corn, venison, and other meat that the Indians kill. In the summer when these kinds of meat are lacking, bear fat is provided to be put into the corn instead of meat. This food will be provided by the merchants who obtain the congés of these posts. For the sick, they will provide the bread and the wine. From all this there will be a set price that will be determined by the average of the highest and lowest prices that deer, a bushel of Indian corn, a hundredweight of flour, a *pot* of wine, are worth at Detroit. Bread for the sick can be provided on the basis of 12 livres per hundredweight of refined flour with only the bran removed, [and] wine at 30 sols[80] per *pot*. For the food of the soldiers who are not sick, a bushel of Indian corn can be furnished for 6 to 7 livres, a whole deer for 9 to 10 livres, a pound of bear fat for 15 sols.

The ordinary ration is one bushel of Indian corn per month for each man, one and one-half pounds of venison or other undomesticated meat per day for each man. When there are no more of these meats or none NAC 2948 can be had, fat is given out. The ration [of fat] is seven and one-half pounds per month for each man.

For the sick the bread ration for one soldier is one and one-half pounds and the ordinary meat, and for a habitant the same quantity. Wine for the former and the latter is one and one-half *setiers*[81] per day. This is the basis on which the bidding is to be carried out.

The king would secure from this a very substantial savings in transport costs. These savings consist of bark canoes that cost new 300# each; wages 156v for the voyageurs to man these canoes; five men per canoe are necessary; the guides of each canoe who are the man in the bow and the one in the stern are paid 250#; the three men in the middle are each paid 200#; the trip is for three months; the supplies for each man in biscuit, bacon, brandy, tobacco, powder, and lead each month are worth 45# at today's prices. At least 60 canoes would be necessary. It is true that a canoe lasts 4 to 5 years when it is well taken care of. At least 30# of equipment are necessary for each canoe; it lasts at least as long as the canoes and consists

NAC 2949 of a kettle, a sail, a large sponge per canoe, gum and 8atape [ouatape; wat-
ape][82] to repair them on the way. This expense would cost 122,160# the
first year, out of which 19,800# must be deducted for the purchase of
canoes and their equipment. The surplus is the annual expense. Every 4 or
5 years it would cost as much as the first year. This expense is for deter-
mining the fees for transporting the food and other provisions of La
Présentation, Fort Frontenac, Toronteaux, and Niagara, and for transporting the trade goods.[83] Add to it the maintenance of the *batteaux du cent*
which carry these items, that of the barks, the wages and food of the
sailors who transport them through Lake Ontario. Even if the king
exploited the posts of which we have just spoken for the trade only, it
would be very wise to have the garrisons' food furnished by the Detroit
157r merchants by competitive bid.

III

The garrisons of the posts of the Belle Rivière will be taken from
the Detroit companies. If soldiers were placed at the Miami and 8ÿatanon
posts, they will be [*sic*] taken from the Detroit companies which will
preferably always be at full strength at 50 men [each]. In peacetime six
NAC 2950 companies are needed and 10 companies in wartime. At Fort Duquesne
in peacetime 40 soldiers are needed. At Rivière au Boeuf and at
Presqu'Isle 30 in each. In wartime at Fort Duquesne 100 soldiers are
needed and 50 in each of the last two; at the Miami post and the
8ÿatanon 30 in each.

If one does not want to create a new headquarters at Detroit because
of the expense, the headquarters at Trois-Rivières serves no purpose. It
could not be more useless there. One has but to place it at Detroit; it has
already been paid for. It would be necessary to place the king's lieutenant
at Michilimackinac[84] with 4 companies in peacetime and in wartime to
have six there to go wherever the needs of the service required. By means
of all these measures, and especially if the Petit Rapide is established and if
the other passages of which I have spoken are rigorously guarded, I would
stake my life on it that none of the nations will move, that they will stay
calm. The Indians are restless and attack only when they see that one is
not in condition to defend oneself, to resist them and to repel their attacks
and punish them for it. Were they to see all the posts manned with troops
and the passages through which they go to the English closed, they would
be softer than a velvet glove.[85]

Eight-man birchbark canoe. These canoes were over 30 feet long and four and a half feet wide. In 1750 the voyageurs assigned to the bow and stern were paid as much as three-quarters more than those in the middle. The total capacity of one such canoe, including men, supplies, and freight, was over three tons. *Drawing by Dirk Gringuis. Courtesy of Mackinac State Historic Parks,* **Michigan.**

As for the Michilimackinac garrison some will ask me how will it live? I have already said and I say again that a means is known to me to provide for it without any transport costs for the king: If I were the major in command of Michilimackinac or if I were granted the La Baye post as a seigniory I would carry out everything that I said if I were ordered to do so.[86]

Regulation and number of congés that will be given in each post the number of which is proportional to their extent, the number of nations, the purpose of the trade that is done and can be done in each.

157v
NAC 2951

Northern Posts

	livres	sols	deniers
Themiskamingue 5 congés	5,000		
Michilimakinac, its dependencies, all of Lake Huron and what is dependent on it, the exclusive trade of the fort 20 congés	20,000		
La Baye, its dependencies, which are the Sac, Fox, Winnebago, Menominee, and Sioux 20 congés	20,000		
The Western Sea, its dependencies, and the Pask8ÿa [Paskoya][87] 20 congés	20,000		
Chagouamigon 16 congés	16,000		
Kamanistigouÿa 10 congés	10,000		

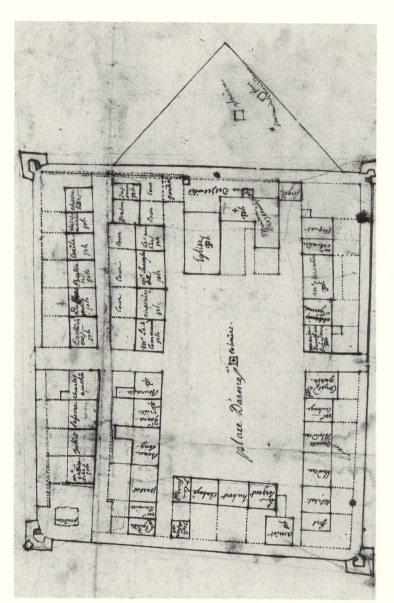

This is the earliest known plan of Michilimackinac, drawn in 1749 by Ensign Michel Chartier de Lotbinière. It shows the parade ground (*place D'armes*) with a crucifix (*calvaire*) in the center. Lotbinière carefully labeled not only the key buildings but wrote the names of the residents (mostly traders) on their houses. *Courtesy of National Archives of Canada, NMC-12806.*

Nepigon 7 congés 7,000
Michipicotton 4 congés 4,000
St. Joseph 7 congés 7,000
The Illinois River from Masanne[88] as
far as the Mississipi [*sic*] River, the
Missoury 20 congés .20,000

129,000#

The merchants who purchase the
congés for Michipicotton and for the
Illinois River having nothing to
carry to Michipicotton nor to
the officers of the Illinois post or
Fort de Chartres[89] will carry equal
portions as far as Michilimakinac and
St. Joseph.

NAC 2952

158r

Southern Posts

At Misiskouÿ[90] and all of Lake
Champlain where the Abenaqui
[Abenaki] and Yrocois go hunting,
three congés 3,000

The Lake of the Two Mountains,
which has up to the present served
only to make such a great fortune
for several peasants whom I know
that there are some who have brought
in this year 1754 for huge sums
silverware in the form of vessels
and platters; all the beaver that
they acquire is taken to the English
who pay them five hundred sols per
pound and they bring back from them
cloth and other prohibited goods in
abundance; they sell this cloth to
the voyageurs of the upper country

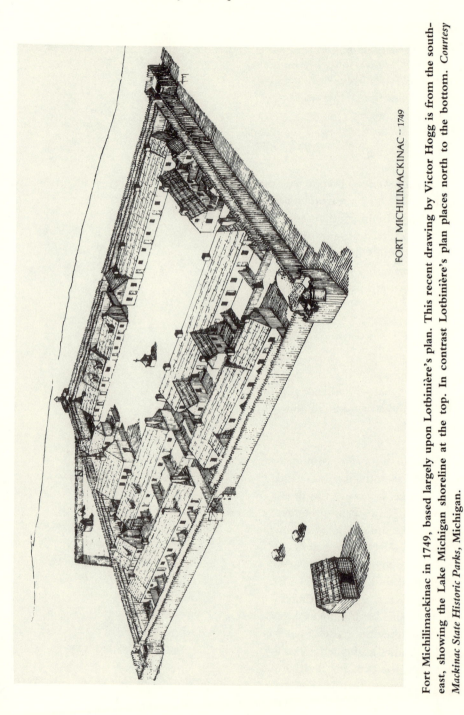

FORT MICHILIMACKINAC -- 1749

Fort Michilimackinac in 1749, based largely upon Lotbinière's plan. This recent drawing by Victor Hogg is from the south-east, showing the Lake Michigan shoreline at the top. In contrast Lotbinière's plan places north to the bottom. *Courtesy Mackinac State Historic Parks, Michigan.*

and have the Indians carry it above
the Long Saut to avoid their being
inspected.[91] Messrs. the priests   NAC 2953
of Montreal will be able to oppose
the king's establishing congés at
the Lake of the Two Mountains,
although he is the master, because
they are being remunerated from it.
The general good of a country's
trade and the king's interests being
preferable to private interests, it
is necessary to establish there six
congés 6,000

At La Présentation one congé 1,000

Fort Frontenac, Toronteaux,
Niagara, that is to say all of Lake
Hontario; the 5 nations if the
merchants who purchase these congés
want to go there twenty   **158v**
congés 20,000

       Detroit, all the posts of the
Belle Rivière and dependencies as
far as the Mississipi River 25
congés 25,000

       The Miami, Tepiconnaud
[Tippecanoe][92] and Coeur de Cerf
[Elkhart, Indiana][93] 6 congés 6,000

       The 8ÿatanon and their
dependencies 8 congés .8,000
                               ———————
                            198,000#

In the Acadian region six congés can be placed. I believe that that
could be worth more, namely at the St. John River which is Father   NAC 2954
Germain's mission,[94] at Monsieur Le Loutre's.[95] It is this abbé who

participates in the trading with the Indians at the St. John River. He is the officer who is in command in that region. All the beaver that comes out of that part of Acadia is taken to the English, who pay over one hundred sols a pound for it. Why not combine this trade with Canada's, since this region costs the king prodigious amounts? Why wouldn't His Majesty benefit as much as possible from it in order to help pay for the expense that it causes him?

Why not farm out the seal- and sea-cow-fishing posts to merchants instead of giving them as pure gifts to private parties? What kind of service are these people giving the king to grant them posts that produce

159r every year 14 and 15 hundred barrels of oil and 3 and 4 thousand seal-skins, which means, in good times or bad, 40, 50, 60, 70, and 80 thousand francs? Take out half of it for expenses, the remainder is considerable. Why not farm out these posts which would give a good income to the king and would help pay the expenses?

NAC 2955 ***I have spoken** to you about the great harm the English are doing to the Canadian trade by the one they are conducting in brandy at Chouagain which is drawing all our Indians to them from all parts of the upper country. Observe that we can increase our trade from everything that leaves our country to go over to them. They profit from it and corrupt our Indians. Note then that we can cause that trade to fail completely and remove from all our nations, as I have already said, any possibility of going any longer to the English. To accomplish that there are two infallible means that I am putting forward here. The first is to guard rigorously the three passages of which I have spoken to you, particularly the Petit Rapide, which must be established because it closes Lake Herrier and in closing it you block and keep in check all your nations; the second means which seems to be inseparable from the first is to allow complete freedom of conscience for all our merchant-voyageurs—whether you give them congés for your posts or you leave things as they are—to trade brandy in all the posts in general; to bother no one about this matter. Let them do it if they want to do it, and do not force them to do it if they do not want

159v to; and to prevent anyone from profiting from the weakness the Indians have for brandy, in order for them not to be swindled, order the price to be established according to the expense brought about by the distance [the

NAC 2956 brandy is transported] and [to] the honest profit the merchants should make. Punish with heavy fines those who exceed the price established by the general, [and] order the commandants to supervise this strictly on pain of losing their supplemental pay.

As soon as our Indians find brandy at home they will not leave to go seek any very far from their village. If they do leave it, since they would find some in all our posts which are on their way, they would buy some there because of their desire to drink, all their furs would be traded at our places before traveling halfway to the English. No longer having anything to bring them, what would they go there for? It is therefore very certain that only these two means would prevent our nations from going out of their territory to go to the English; they would never be in a position to go there.

Messrs. the bishops of Canada, at the solicitation of the missionaries, have preached and had it preached that this brandy trade was such an enormous crime that it was irremissible. They made it a case of conscience reserved to them for being absolved from it. Our merchants, to avoid the hell that was opening up under their feet, have given up this trade. The generals, upon the bishop's pastorals forbidding it, also prohibited it.

Since that time, our Indians who did not previously go to the English NAC 2957 have always gone to them.

For several years it has been traded (on the king's account and to his **160r** profit, at least that is what we are told) in the posts of Forts Frontenac, Toronteaux, and Niagara. The ecclesiastical power and the country's government have however from time to time obligingly eased the severity of their prohibition for M. de Laperade who traded it when he had the Miami post; for M. Marin, Senior who, during all of these recent years, sold it at La Baye; for his son who is presently selling it in this same post; for the eldest Repentigny son who had the St. Joseph post 4 years ago; for the Chevalier de Repentigny who has Saut Ste. Marie from M. De Bonne; and finally for M. de St. Pierre who has just left the Western Sea and for the Chevalier de La Corne who is presently there.[96] Why has this brandy trade been tolerated for these gentlemen and forbidden to all the merchants with so much severity? If it is such a great crime as they say, there must be no special treatment for anyone. It is made a crime, a prohibition, a reserved case[97] for me, and not for you. If it is a great sin, it is a sin for you as it is for me. If it is recognized and judged with certain knowledge that it is an evil which must be extinguished, it must not be NAC 2958 done by whoever it might be. The prohibition must in general be for every kind of person without distinction. The general interest and God's cause must not allow preferential treatment for anyone.[98] In the future, then, let it be determined to prohibit the brandy trade irrevocably or let it be open to all those who want to engage in it, and let it no longer be made a case reserved to the bishops, and let all the confessionals be open to the penitents.

160v   If it is resolved to prohibit this trade let it be tolerated no longer by anyone and let the first one who sells any to the Indians be hanged.**

Regulation of the supplementary pay of the commanding and junior officers assigned to all the posts; of the captains and officers garrisoned at Detroit and at Michilimakinac if they are placed there; of the chaplains and surgeons assigned; and other expenses.

To wit

To the captains of the following 4 posts:

Fort Frontenac ⎫
Niagara   ⎬   6,000# to each . . . . .24,000#
Detroit   ⎪
Michilimakinac ⎭

For the 4 lieutenants, their
seconds, the sum of 3,000
to the missionary 600
to the surgeon 600

NAC 2959 **Fort** Frontenac and Niagara for the
other junior officers and other
expenses for the two:
2 full ensigns, to each 1,500# . . . . .3,000#
2 second ensigns, to each 1,200# 2,400
2 chaplains, to each 600# 1,200
2 surgeons fed, and to each 300# 600
2 carters at 400# each, half charged
to the king 400
2 cowherds, to each 150# 300
3 thousand of hay for each fort at one
hundred écus [300#] per thousand, half
charged to the king 900
4 hundred cords of wood at 25 sols for
each fort, for both of them 1,000

                                                    ‾‾‾‾‾‾‾
                                                    38,000#

For chimney sweeping of each fort
and placing the flag there and sweeping
the corridors, for each, 200#, totalling. 400

For the captains in command of all the other
posts of the upper country and their seconds-
in-command:

To wit

Presqu'isle	new settlements
Rivière au boeuf	of the
Fort Duquesne	Belle Rivière

Miami
8ÿatanon
La Baye

La Mer du ouest
Chaoüamigon
Kamanistigouÿa
Nepigon
St. Joseph

   Six captains that would be needed
with their complete companies of
50 men as a garrison at Detroit.
For the 17 above captains commanding
garrisons,[99] 3,000# per year each as
supplementary pay, totalling 51,000
   For the 11 lieutenants second-in-
command and six of the aforesaid
garrison companies, at 2,000# each,
totalling 34,000
To the six full ensigns of
the aforesaid companies, at 1,500#
each 9,000
To the six second ensigns at 1,200#
each 7,200

  At Fort Chambly only a caretaker is
needed. If an officer is desired, he
needs no soldiers. He will be provided
with no food and will be given 1,000# of
supplementary pay. He will be a junior
officer. 1,000

                                        ——————
                                        140,600#

161v **Fort St. Frédéric** [Marginal note:
Nothing will be furnished, neither food
nor gear, to the commandants.]
1 commandant 3,000
1 lieutenant, second-in-command 1,500
1 full ensign at 1,200#, totalling 1,200
NAC 2961 1 second ensign 1,000# totalling 1,000
1 chaplain at 300# totalling 300
1 surgeon at 300# totalling 300
1 baker at 300# totalling .300
1 carter at 400# totalling .400
1 cowherd at 150# totalling 150
1 blacksmith at 400# totalling 400
1 clerk to distribute the food, at 500
3 thousand of hay at 300# per thousand 900
400 cords of wood at 25 sols 500

        St. Jean
1 lieutenant as commandant, for his
supplementary pay 1,500
1 second ensign, as second-in-command,
totalling 1,000
1 baker at 300# 300
1 carter at 300
1 clerk to distribute the food 600
2 thousand hay at 300#, totalling 600
100 cords of wood at 25 sols, totalling   <u>125</u>

                                        ——————
                                        <u>155,575</u>

In these two forts rations will continue
to be given, with the exception of the
commandant of Fort St. Frédéric, who has the
same supplementary pay as the officers in
command of the other posts who have no
expenditures to make.

At La Présentation it is pointless to
assign either a commandant or troops.
If an officer is desired to be kept
there a lieutenant can be placed
there. He will be provided with
neither food nor gear. He will be
given only 2,000# of supplementary pay,
totalling 2,000

NAC 2962

162r

_____

157,575#

We have seen that the congés to be
established in the posts and where it
is appropriate have produced the sum of . . . . . . .198,000#

We also see that the supplementary pay
of all the commandants and officers
serving in all the posts and garrisons,
that of the chaplains, the wages of the
surgeons and other employees, and other
expenses of the garrisons of Forts
Frontenac, Niagara, St. Frédéric, and
St. Jean, all of it taken out of the
amount produced from the congés, adds
up to 157,575

_____

Leaving the sum of   40,425#

Observe, then, my dear Sur la Ville that all the service expenses of all
the posts and of all the garrisons are paid without costing the king anything, and that forty thousand four hundred twenty-five livres remaining
after the expenses are paid come into the king's coffers by means of the

NAC 2963

project that I am recommending to you and that I would put into operation if I had the authority, in order to serve the king, my master, well. You ask me what the soldiers who are garrisoned at these posts cost the king. They cost nothing. The posts' garrisons, like those in the towns, pay for their food. Five livres per month are withheld from their pay, by means of which the expense of the food that is furnished to them comes in almost entirely.[100]

162v

As to the peas needed for the garrisons and the oats for the horses of Forts St. Frédéric, St. Jean, Fort Frontenac, Toronteaux, and Niagara, the commandants have to do as I did when I was in command in these garrisons. The horses and harnesses being the king's and the land all prepared, let them sow profusely peas and oats. They will gather more than will be consumed, which will spare the king the cost of purchasing and transporting them.

If chaplains are placed in the Belle Rivière forts, they will be given, like those at Detroit, 600# and, like them, they will be brought their provisions that they will pay for out of their supplementary pay. The surgeons, if they are placed there, will be treated as I said in the section on the regulation of what must be brought to each one.

NAC 2964

If the merchants do not furnish the food and it is the king, a steward will be needed at Forts Frontenac, Toronteaux, Niagara to distribute it. Having but this one job to do, ordinary rations and wages of 300# will be given to them. To avoid this expense the commandant can have them distributed by a sergeant in the garrison to whom 100# would be given to each for their trouble. At each fort a baker will also be needed. If the merchants make use of them they will feed and pay them, half-and-half with the king.

163r

If companies were to be placed in a garrison at Michilimakinac, the captains and their officers will be treated like those in the Detroit garrison. These last expenses will be taken out of the 40,425# remaining in the amount produced by the congés.

*I have spoken only in an offhand way about La Présentation,[101] established for several years 25 or 30 leagues above Montreal on the Frontenac River [the upper St. Lawrence River] at the place called La Galete [La Galette], halfway to that fort [Frontenac] and on the way to it. Its large building, the sawmills, the clearing of much land have cost the king considerable sums and presently cost annually a great amount of money for its maintenance; for supplementary pay, wages, food, charges, and expense for the transporting of the food and other provisions for the

NAC 2965

officers, soldiers, quartermasters, bakers, carters, blacksmiths, surgeons, and a great number of useless people; the clothing and annual food of all the Indians that are assembled there.

This settlement was created however only by the entreaties, only by the demands of Abbé Piquet, who, through his maneuvering, his rubrics, and all the motivating forces that he put into play with highly placed people to have his proposal accepted, succeeded in having it ordained. All those people in Canada who are sensible and who think clearly have not been able to understand what good and what advantage made known by Abbé Piquet could be drawn from it for the king's service and the colony. It is then doubtlessly for the glory of religion and the zeal to 163v make Christians. Charitably I would like to believe it. It would have been easier and a more certain means for Abbé Piquet to satisfy his zeal by remaining in his mission where he was at the Lake of the Two Mountains,[102] where there is a village of Algonquin, one of Nepissing, and one of Irocois, to make use of these converted Indians to attract the Five Nations to religion. The example and the prayers of the latter would have brought them to their brothers at this mission if they had wanted to become Christians. Have the Jesuit fathers who have incomparable zeal for making Christians ever been able to attract the Five Nations with their blood brothers to their mission of the Saut?[103] You ask me, the Five NAC 2966 Nations have not yielded then to the apostolic voice of Abbé Piquet? No, they have not yielded and will not yield to it. There is only a collection of old women, old men, wild young Indian women who were chased from their villages because of their debauchery, libertines, womanizers who follow them. And among all those people, there is no family, nor any chief held in esteem who inspires confidence among the Five Nations. They only stay on at La Présentation because the king feeds and dresses them there; let them be given nothing more, none will remain there.

La Présentation several years from now will be requested by Messrs. de St. Sulpice as a grant. Abbé Piquet's zeal in wanting to make Christians will end up making beautiful lands, most of which will be 164r completely cleared, and all that at the king's expense. That is what is called a true apostle who is most zealous for the glory of God. The money that La Présentation has cost would have been much better used to place settlers at Detroit. The money that it will cost would be better spent there or used for the expense of your new Belle Rivière posts in order to keep them for ourselves, but you are not warning me that in NAC 2967

Portrait of Abbé François Picquet (1708-81). Prior to his establishing the post of La Présentation, this colorful Sulpician priest lived at the mission of Lac-des-Deux-Montagnes (Oka, Quebec) from 1739 to 1749 and briefly in 1758. He distinguished himself in battle during the French and Indian War. This portrait was located in 1997 in the presbytery of the Paroisse de l'Annonciation of Oka. *Reproduced courtesy of Les Prêtres de Saint-Sulpice - Oka.*

giving you a detailed account of Canada I am running the risk of being excommunicated and making irreconcilable enemies for myself for speaking about La Présentation and Abbé Piquet. I see a host of enemies that you are going to draw to me because of all the truths that you are having me bring to light solely to satisfy your curiosity. I am determined to no longer say anything to you; I will say no more other than the observation that follows before giving you the details of the present and annual expenses saved by carrying out the project in this report, and that is where I shall end.★★

I note that there are unexpected circumstances in the service that oblige the commanders to make speeches. They call it making speeches when they assemble them [the Indians] to speak to them, for the good of the service, or during those occasions when they need to use them for the service. They give them wampum belts about which I have already spoken and some of all the goods that they use. These occasions occur again when it is necessary to cover their dead, or to raise them up from their mourning. Covering the dead is when the wife or the children or the parents of a great chief happen to die or when they are killed in their warfare, or when these great chiefs happen to die, or to be killed themselves. They give to NAC 2968 these chiefs, or after their death to their widows and children, the kind of 164v presents of which I have spoken above following a speech that they give them to exhort them to do what they require of them or following a condolence speech upon the occasion of the deaths. They give these presents again a year after the demise of their dead. That is what they call raising them up from their mourning. They give them these presents, they also make a speech to finish consoling them and to call upon them not to take up any more of their time with their affliction. These are rules of conduct observed among the Indians which we are obliged to follow with them.[104]

In all these cases [of giving presents to the Indians] the commandants will take from the merchants who hold the posts' congés the necessary goods that they will not be able to refuse to provide upon the commandants' orders and who will be paid for them at 50 percent above the price of their being fitted out by His Majesty. Where there are missionaries at the posts they will attend these councils and will be present when the commandants give these speeches or presents to the Indians, or when they respond at the councils that they have come to hold at your [*sic*] place, and will validate the certificates in writing that the commandants give to the merchants to be used for their payment which will be made without being reduced.[105] This precaution is only to avoid the abuses NAC 2969 that are committed by those favored commandants who themselves furnish the merchandise on these occasions, who create it when there is

165r none, who put down exorbitant prices for their merchandise in bills for supplies under assumed names. These bills, in many of the posts that I know even now, go beyond 30 and 40 thousand francs a year. How could they make such quick fortunes if they were not dipping into the king's purse? Will you say that these posts must not have commandants whose honor, probity, and conscience are not recognized as being incapable of swindling the king, of abusing the trust placed in them and the powers given to them? Are you to expect this probity in these favored commandants who are as greedy for money as those with whom they are partners? Those who have the greatest ability to benefit from it [i.e., command of a post] and to have a great deal produced from it are the meritorious, able, knowledgeable officers who have been praised, who deserve the king's favor and their promotion.

NAC 2970   [As for] **the presents** that the Indians can give to the commandants, if they are furs, they will reciprocate with goods from the merchants, taking care to give them some only of equal value, on the basis of the fur trade, and the furs will be given to the merchants. If that is not suitable to them, the commandants will pay their account and the furs will remain with them.

★**As** it is necessary from time to time to give presents to the Indians in order to make them faithful to us, and as there is a fund for that purpose, those destined for them will be taken from the king's storehouses and will be apportioned according to the number of each post's Indians. They will be delivered by the merchants. The commandants will distribute them in the presence of the missionaries, who will be notified of

165v what will be sent, and when they are distributed to the Indians an accounting will be made of them which will be certified by the missionaries as to what quantity they have received. And where there are no missionaries, the merchants in charge[106] will certify it. This precaution is offensive only to the scoundrels who are obsessed with vile gain. The commandants who are mindful of their probity, who would be distressed to think that it could be suspect, would never be offended by this formality. On the contrary, they would have to be delighted with it, since

NAC 2971 all those who are led only by the hand of justice and equity know as I do what has happened and is happening, what has been said, and what is still being said today about these favorites, about these partnerships past and present which have caused and still cause all of Canada to groan,

Copy of a portrait of Jacques-Pierre de Taffanel de La Jonquière, Governor General of New France, 1749-1752. *Copy done in the 1930s by C. W. Jefferys from an unknown source. Reproduced by permission of the National Archives of Canada, C-69302.*

particularly all of the country's merchants whose cries and complaints have crossed over the seas.[107] Let us not leave our upper country. What haven't we seen going out of the king's stores that was intended as presents for the Indians but which served only to fatten the purse of many people and help make their fortune? And yet they make a crime out of what one says, for what one sees, and for knowing everything they do. Those who speak about it are proscribed, ill-served. Hey! For how long have they been causing the ruin of those who speak and expose the truth to those who, in order to set everything right, would find it interesting to see?

Since you want things right, it would be especially necessary to forbid all commandants and junior officers in the posts to engage, or have anyone engage, directly or indirectly in any trading. Those proved to have traded will lose their supplementary pay, will receive one year in prison, and will come out only to be reduced to the ranks at the head of the troops without ever being able to reenter the service. The commandants and junior officers will be relieved every three years in order for all the officers to be able to profit successively from this supplementary pay to put them equally in condition to live and sustain their service with all the honor and dignity it requires, which will never be, and always the king will be ill-served, so long as all favors are given to some and so long as most of the officer corps have no bread and are on the streets.★★

Before placing before your eyes the present cost of provisioning the garrisons whose expense would be saved by means of carrying out the present report, to make it [the expense] clearer it is first necessary to go into the details of the rations that are distributed daily, basing their price on what they cost the king delivered at the locations and on what the king has those pay who take some beyond what is given to them, and what they sell for to the voyageurs and Indians who stop at the king's storehouse. The habitant's ration is 2 lbs. of bread per day, which makes 60 lbs. per month which is reduced to 10 six-pound loaves. This bread sells for 20 sols to those who take some beyond their ration and [the habitant's ration includes] 1/2 lb. of bacon per day which makes 15 lbs. per month; a pound sells for 10 sols although the suppliers have the king pay 15 sols. Brandy at the king's storehouse sells for 6# per *pot*, wine for 3#, powder for 30 sols, lead for 15 sols, tobacco for 20 sols per pound, peas for 6# per bushel. It is on the basis of all these prices that you are going to see the annual value of the food for each person the king feeds and this is what will let you see the savings.

166r

NAC 2972

NAC 2973

166v

M. *François Bigot, the Intendant.*

Caricature of Michel Bigot, Intendant of New France, 1748–60. *Reproduced with permission of the National Archives of Canada, C-3715.*

We have said that the officers and chaplains of Forts Frontenac and Niagara would feed themselves by means of the supplementary pay that would be paid to them, that there was no need for a garrison at La Présentation, that at Toronteaux there would only be a detachment during the summer taken from the garrison of Fort Frontenac. We have also said that the king would no longer need a storekeeper, interpreter, bakers, blacksmiths; that the officers' supplementary pay, the employees' wages, the expense for hay, firewood, chimney sweeping, that all the aforesaid expenses would no longer come from the king's coffers; that they would be taken out of the fund that we have created from the income from the congés for Forts St. Frédéric, St. Jean, Chambly, Fort Frontenac, Niagara, and La Présentation if a commandant is desired there.

Present annual **salaries** at the aforesaid garrisons:

NAC 2974 **Savings:**

7 commandants at 600# of supplementary
pay per year for each, totalling . . . . .4,200#
7 storekeepers (2 at Niagara) at
600# in wages per year for each. 4,200
3 chaplains at 300# totalling 900
4 surgeons at 300# totalling 1,200
6 bakers at 400# totalling 2,400
6 blacksmiths at 400# totalling 2,400
6 carters at 400# totalling 2,400

167r 3 interpreters at 500# totalling 1,500

for 4 forts {
3 cowherds at 150# totalling 450
11 thousand of hay at 300# per thousand . .3,300
13 hundred cords of wood at 25^s totalling. .1,625
chimney cleaning and flag 700
}

Supplementary pay given annually to the
junior officers of Forts Frontenac and Niagara,
for those at these two forts only 1,200# 1,200

_____

26,475#

Rations, To Wit:
For each commandant and storekeeper 72 lb.
of bread and 15 lb. of bacon per month; for one

year 144 6-lb. loaves, 180 lbs. of bacon, a barrel
of wine, 24 *pots* of brandy, 12 *pots* of vinegar, 12
pots of molasses, 2 bushels of peas, 15 lbs. of
powder, 30 lbs. of lead, 15 lbs. of candles, 20 lbs. of butter (the
storekeepers have as many candles as they want,
and with butter), 6 lbs. of sugar,[108] 1 1/2 lbs.
of pepper.

NAC 2975

   As for bread and bacon, the junior officers
have as much as the commandants; as to the rest
and all the lesser provisions, they have only
half of what the commandants have.

6 commandants, for bread, totalling . . . . .864#
for bacon, totalling 540
6 barrels of wine at 120# totalling 720
144 *pots* of brandy at 6#, totalling 864
72 *pots* of vinegar at 3# totalling. 216
72 *pots* of molasses at 2# totalling. 144
12 bushels of peas at 6# totalling. 72
90 lbs. of powder at 30 sols totalling 135
180 lbs. of lead at 15 sols totalling 135
90 lbs. of candles at 15 sols totalling. 67
120 lbs. of butter at 15 sols totalling. 90
144 lbs. of white sugar at 20 sols 144
9 lbs. of pepper at 3#. 27
for the bread of their six servants totalling 720
for the bacon for the six 540
9 bushels of peas for the six 54
For the rations of the six wives of the six
commandants:
for their bread each year for the six 864
for the bacon of the six 540

167v

NAC 2976

   Separate out the supplementary pay of the six
commandants, their rations, those of their servants,
those of their wives; that makes a total of 10,841#.
Add to the present account the same amount for the
six storekeepers, their six valets, and their six

wives because they have the same provisions as the
commandants:

　　　　　for the aforesaid storekeepers, their valets
and wives, totalling. .10,841
⎧ for the bread and bacon of 12 junior officers
⎨ totalling 2,808
⎩ they have as much as the commandants
for the other lesser provisions having only half
of what the commandants have, totalling 1,274

for 4 chaplains
bread 576
bacon 360
2 barrels of wine at 120# 240
96 *pots* of brandy at 6#. 576

168r　48 *pots* of vinegar at 3# totalling 144
48 *pots* of molasses at 2# totalling 96
8 bushels of peas at 6# totalling 48
60 lbs. of powder at 15 sols 90
120 lbs. of lead at 15 sols totalling 90

NAC 2977　60 lbs. of candles at 15 sols totalling 45
80 lbs. of butter at 15 *sols* totalling 60
24 lbs. of white sugar at 20 sols 24
6 lbs. of pepper at 3# 18

for 4 interpreters
bread 480
bacon 360
48 *pots* of brandy at 6# 288
48 lbs. of tobacco at 20 sols totalling 48
6 bushels of peas at 6# totalling 36

for 4 surgeons
the same amount, making 1,212# totalling 1,212

for 6 bakers
6 bakers for the bread for the six 720
bacon totalling 540
72 *pots* of brandy at 6# totalling 432

72 lbs. of tobacco at 20 *sols* totalling 72
9 bushels of peas at 6# totalling. 54
for 6 blacksmiths the same amount, which
makes 1,818# totalling .1,818
for 6 carters the same amount, which makes. 1,818
for 4 cowherds the same amount of rations
as the 4 surgeons, which makes 1,212
The surgeons, bakers, blacksmiths, and
carters ordinarily have their wives with them
to whom the same rations as their husband are given,
which adds a considerable expense.

168v

NAC 2978

2 Barks

2 masters at 600# per year 1,200
10 sailors at 25# per month which makes one
hundred écus per year for the 10
totalling 3,000# 3,000
masters and sailors 12 people; they have the
same rations as the other employees above,
which for the 12 per year totals 3,636

      For the transportation of all the food
and other provisions that are hauled by cart
from Montreal as far as Lachine, what it
costs is not known to me, but that must be a
considerable amount. It must go beyond at
least 25 or 30 thousand livres. I am
estimating it approximately. From Lachine
the *batteaux du cent* carry them to La
Présentation and to Fort Frontenac. Those
that are entrusted with piloting the boats
are paid today by the thousand [weight] at
the rate of 4# 10 sols per hundredweight.
Each boat carries from 6 to 8 thousand pounds
of weight. Each trip includes 15 boats. 5
to 6 trips are taken

NAC 2979

Barks on the St. Lawrence, ca. 1683. *Detail from "Québec," Alain Manesson Mallet's etching in* **Description** *de* l'univers *(Paris, 1683)5: 277. Reproduced with permission of the National Archives of Canada, C-107626.*

each year. That is an expenditure of about
25 thousand francs per year. Figure the
cartage at only 25 thousand francs; that
makes 50,000#, totalling 50,000

    These last two expenditures will surely go
beyond 60 thousand francs.

                                        117,427#

169r

For the expense of transporting goods and
food to the Belle Rivière amounting to the
sum of 60,000#, totalling 60,000

For the spoiled bacon and other food that
end up as a pure loss for the king,
totalling 6,000

Each *batteaux du cent* costs the king 300#.
This expense, which is considerable, is not
known to me any more than the upkeep of the
barks, costing His Majesty at least 10,000#.

Total of the amount saved for the king . . . . <u>183,427#</u>

    Each year adding up to the total of one hundred eighty-three thousand four hundred twenty-seven livres. Besides the savings of the aforementioned amount, a considerable one would come from [avoiding the NAC 2980 cost of] the loss of flour which occurs in shipping, from flour that spoils, from leakage of wine and brandy which are transported for the Indian trade.

    ★You ask me what profit the king makes from this trade. I shall answer you that a private party would earn a considerable amount, and that His Majesty loses from it, because everybody sees and knows that all the operations, all the work, all the purchases that are done straight from the king's purse and on his account are done without savings, without care, and always with higher charges and higher expenditures than can be arranged for earning more. Those through whose hands these kinds of tasks pass furnish all these supplies themselves under assumed names and have a financial interest in the other expenditures. Those who engage in this trade steal with impunity. I have had under my command storekeep- **169v** ers who had no shoes on their feet when they entered the king's storehouses and who, with 600# in wages given to them annually, left at the end of 5 to 6 years extremely well off. How could they earn so much money if they were not robbing the king, and so many others who are filling themselves up? You ask me if so many abuses and so much expense for the king cannot be remedied. It is precisely to have you see that that NAC 2981 can be done that★★ I have gone with you into all the details that I have presented to you which formed the substance of this present report that you requested of me in order to be able to speak about Canada with full knowledge of the facts. If it were to come before the eyes of the minister as it has before yours, and if he went to the trouble of examining it himself as you are doing, he would open them enough to have it carried out. If I were chosen for that and invested with the powers and authority along with the title of inspector general of the troops, garrisons, and posts of the upper country,[109] I would carry it out. I would collect the receipts from the income from the congés out of which I would pay all the expenses that I have showed you, especially if I were to receive a salary suitable for paying for my lodging, for the expenses that that would bring about for me and for living as would befit the standing of this office, and for being able to incur the expenses that I would be obliged to incur to inspect the garrisons and the posts. As all of this will

170r not happen, I shall finish by telling you that I had you note that the present salary of the posts' commandants that you are asking me about is for those to whom these [trading] posts are given to be disposed of as they

NAC 2982 wish for their profit, which in this case takes the place of supplementary pay for them. [As for] the commandants who are not masters of the [trading] posts where they are in command, [the trade of] these posts being conducted by congés or farmed out,[110] in this case the commandants are given one thousand écus per year as supplementary pay out of which they pay all their expenses.

As for the commandants of Chambly, St. Frédéric, St. Jean, La Présentation, Fort Frontenac, Toronteaux, and Niagara, the king gives them the ration that I showed you and supplementary pay of 600# a year and nothing else. The junior officers of these garrisons have no supplementary pay; it is only those who serve at Fort Frontenac and Niagara who have 1,200# to share among them and the rations that are given to them.

Do not ask me for anything more. I believe I have told you too much. If it were known that I have informed you so well and that I have drawn back the curtain behind which you have seen everything, they would wish me ill, as far as wanting to strangle me. Thus you are obliged to defend me. You are certainly aware that if you had grounds to send this report to be considered in Canada, it would be condemned and the author banished, even if it were to be found to be the best in the world. Anything that does not come from the wisdom of those upon whom one

170v depends is never approved. They make you out to be a fraud.[111] You

NAC 2983 know that better than I. If you expose me to Canadian vengeance, become my protector. You owe it to my friendship for you. Farewell, and let me know your thoughts.

NOTES

1. Raymond's spelling of Surlaville's name in his first sentence announces the level of spelling throughout the report.

2. Antoine-Louis Rouillé, Comte de Jouy, was minister of Marine from 1749 to 1754; Jean-Baptiste Machault d'Arnouville was minister from 1754 to 1757.

3. Temiscaming is about three hundred miles northwest of Montreal, near the headwaters of the Ottawa River. Throughout this translation where the spelling or variants of place names given by Raymond depart from the usual terminology of the period, alternate spellings are provided in brackets. The present English place names are also given in brackets.

4. La Baye in Wisconsin is not to be confused with *La Baye verte* in Acadia, following (NAC 2908).

5. After the Treaty of Utrecht, the French sought to expand their threatened fur trade to the northwest of Lake Superior. In 1717 they founded the post of Kaministiquia on the northwest side of Lake Superior (near Thunder Bay, Ontario), followed by posts established by the La Vérandryes, namely Fort St. Pierre on Rainy Lake in 1731; Fort St. Charles on the Lake of the Woods in 1732; Fort Maurepas on the Red River (near Winnipeg, Manitoba) in 1734; Fort La Reine (Portage la Prairie, Manitoba), just south of Lake Manitoba on the Assiniboine River in 1738; Fort Dauphin (Dauphin, Manitoba), west of Lake Dauphin, and Fort Bourbon at the north of Lake Winnipegosis in 1741; and, in 1743, Fort Paskoya (near Le Pas, Manitoba) on the Saskatchewan to the northwest of Lake Winnipeg, close to today's boundary between the Provinces of Manitoba and Saskatchewan.

   Several other fortified posts were founded by the French in this vast region; the westernmost Fort La Jonquière, was founded by Jacques Legardeur de Saint-Pierre's men in 1751, far to the west of Fort Paskoya. Collectively known as the Post [*sic*] of the Western Sea, these posts vied with the English at Hudson Bay for the high-quality furs in the region (Marcel Trudel, *Initiation à la Nouvelle-France* [Montréal: Les Editions HRW, ltée, 1971], 88-89). See Joseph L. Peyser, *Jacques Legardeur de Saint-Pierre: Officer, Gentleman, Entrepreneur* (East Lansing and Mackinac Island: Michigan State University Press and Mackinac State Historic Parks, 1996), chaps. 5 and 6, for the history of the French presence in this region and for extensive detail on Saint-Pierre's exploration, fur trading, and slave trading at the Western Sea from 1750 to 1753.

6. Louis de Bonne de Missègle, a relative of Governor General La Jonquière (1749-52), arrived in New France in 1749 with the governor. De Bonne was granted, along with Louis Legardeur de Repentigny, the fief of Sault-Ste-Marie in 1750. Legardeur de Repentigny lived at the post. De Bonne was killed in action near Quebec in 1760. See Jean-Marie Leblanc, "Bonne de Missègle (Missèle), Louis de," *Dictionary of Canadian Biography* (hereafter cited as *DCB*), 12 vols. (Toronto: University of Toronto Press, 1966-91), 3:69-70.

7. Chagouamigon, on the south shore of Lake Superior, was one of four important French posts on this lake.

8. Nipigon, Ontario, is on the north shore of Lake Superior, south of Lake Nipigon.

9. Michipicoton is on the northeast shore of Lake Superior.

10. The Saint Joseph River post, less commonly known to the French as Fort St. Joseph, was located about 30 miles inland from the mouth of the St. Joseph River, now Niles, Michigan. This post is not to be confused with La Salle's Miami post (1679-c.1688), which was at the mouth of the Saint Joseph River, or with the Miami post at today's Fort Wayne, Indiana. See Joseph L. Peyser, *Letters from New France: The Upper Country 1686-1783* (Urbana: University of Illinois Press, 1992), 78-81, for the evolution of the name of this post.

11. From 1717 the Illinois country came under the authority of the Louisiana colony. The Ouiatanon post on the Wabash and the St. Joseph River post remained part of New France under the authority of the governor general. Later in his *dénombrement* (157 verso-158 recto; NAC 2951-52) Raymond identifies the approximate boundaries of the Illinois trading territory as well as the substantial volume of Canadian trade there.

    Congés were trade licenses issued by the governor general and visaed by the intendant of New France. For a succinct overview of New France's congé system from 1681 to the Conquest, see Peyser, *Jacques Legardeur de Saint-Pierre*, 6-8 and passim.

12. The term Raymond used is *la grande rivierre*.

13. A league is 2.42 miles.

14. *La Présentation*, Presentation in English, is a Catholic religious observance on 21 November celebrating the presentation of the Virgin Mary in the temple. The post was located at today's Ogdensburg, New York, on the upper St. Lawrence River. François Picquet, a Sulpician priest and missionary, founded La Présentation in 1749, where he had a fort and living quarters built that housed about three hundred Iroquois and Huron. Raymond comments extensively on Picquet and this post on folios 163 recto to 164 recto (NAC transcript pp. 2965-67), following. See Robert Lahaise, "Picquet, François," *DCB*, 4:636-37 for details on the colorful and controversial abbé.

15. See note 11 above. Raymond's term *au dessus*, here translated as "beyond," literally means "above" in the sense of "farther up" in the upper country, even though the posts he is referring to (Vincennes and Fort de Chartres) are to the south and southwest of the Ouiatanon post.

16. For information on the development of Fort Chambly and life at the post see Cyrille Gélinsas, *The Role of Fort Chambly in the Development of New France*, Studies in Archaeology, Architecture and History (hereafter cited as SAAH) (Ottawa: Canadian Parks Service, 1983); François Miville-Deschênes, *The Soldier Off Duty: Domestic Aspects of Military Life at Fort Chambly under the French Régime as Revealed by Archaeological Objects*, SAAH (Ottawa: Canadian Parks Service, 1987); Pierre

Beaudet and Céline Cloutier, *Archaeology at Fort Chambly*, SAAH (Ottawa: Canadian Parks Service, 1989).

17. The French began the occupation and fortification of Crown Point, New York, which they called Fort St. Frédéric, in 1731. In 1755, less than 10 miles to the south, on a neck of land between Lake Champlain and Lake George, the French began the construction of Fort Carillon, later called Ticonderoga. These forts were major obstacles to British invasion attempts from the south, as well as staging areas for French assaults on the British colonies.

18. The term *batteaux* was used here by Raymond. A *bateau* could be any boat, large or small, but in this context it probably meant a flat-bottomed boat used for river travel. John Francis McDermott defined a *bateau plat* as a "light flat boat, sharp of bow and stern, of light draft and narrow beam." He described a number of these ordered for the Mississippi River as being "40 by 9 by 4 feet, each of 12 tons burden" (*A Glossary of Mississippi Valley French 1673-1850*, New Series, Language and Literature, No. 12 [St. Louis: Washington University Studies, 1941], 20). Peter Kalm described the Albany, New York, "battoes" that were mainly used for carrying goods along rivers to the Indians. They were "sharp at both ends," had seats in them, were rowed "as common boats," and were from three to four fathoms (18 to 24 feet) long. Their height "from the bottom to the top of the board" was from 20 inches to 2 feet, and their width at the center was about 42 inches (Peter Kalm, *Travels in North America*, ed. Adolph B. Benson, 2 vols. [New York: Dover Publications, Inc., 1964], 1:333. Five bateaux dating from the early 1750s excavated at Quebec in 1985-86 averaged 33 feet in length (Kevin J. Crisman, "Struggle for a Continent: Naval Battles of the French and Indian Wars," in *Ships and Shipwrecks of the Americas: A History Based on Underwater Archaeology* [New York: Thames and Hudson, 1988], 132-33). See also notes 56 and 58, below.

19. Laprairie is on the other side of the St. Lawrence River from the island of Montreal, to the southeast. Sault St. Louis was the location of a Jesuit mission for Christian Iroquois across the St. Lawrence to the south of Montreal. The Lake of Two Mountains (Lac des Deux Montagnes) was the location of a Sulpician mission for Christian Iroquois and Algonquins across the lake to the west of Montreal, at Oka. The French-allied resident Iroquois warriors fought in battle alongside the French on various occasions, including, for example, the 40 Iroquois accompanying Pierre d'Artaguiette and François-Marie Bissot de Vincennes's forces from Upper Louisiana in the ill-fated 1736 attack against the Chickasaw village, and the Christian Mohawks serving with Jacques Legardeur de Saint-Pierre under General Jean-Armand Dieskau in 1755 at the Battle of Lake George.

20. Raymond is writing here about the governor generals, who individually were commonly referred to simply as "the general" by the officers.

21. Raymond's rather understated comment about officers' pretty wives is accurate. Among others, he was undoubtedly thinking of Michel-Jean-Hugues Péan, an unprincipled officer and entrepreneur whose wife was the mistress of François

Bigot, the powerful intendant of New France (Gaston Du Boscq de Beaumont, *Les derniers jours de l'Acadie (1748-1758)*: *Correspondances et mémoires* [Paris: 1899; reprint Geneva: Slatkine-Megariotis Reprints, 1975], 9; Henri-Raymond Casgrain, *Guerre du Canada, 1756-1760, Montcalm et Lévis*, 2 vols. [Québec: Demers et Frères, 1891], 1:314). Péan became a major partner of Bigot in dishonest large-scale transactions. For the exchange of favors between such officers and their wives on the one hand, and the highly placed administrators on the other, see J. F. Bosher and J.-C. Dubé, "Bigot, François," *DCB*, 4:65; Guy Dinel, "Péan, Michel-Jean-Hugues," *DCB*, 4:615; and Pierre Pouchot, *Memoirs On The Late War in North America Between France and England*, trans. Michael Cardy and ed. Brian Leigh Dunnigan (Youngstown, N.Y.: Old Fort Niagara Publications, 1994), 60-61, 63, 321.

22. The "last war" mentioned here by Raymond was King George's War. For details on the so-called "Huron Conspiracy," viewed by the French as a general uprising of the Indians, see Part I, pp. 17-19 and 24-26, of this work, and Peyser, *Jacques Legardeur de Saint-Pierre*, 87-88 and 91-111 passim.

23. The Indians called the governor generals *Onontio* and the French kings *Great Onontio*. Raymond wrote here *le grand aunonthio*, meaning Louis XV.

24. Here Raymond wrote *ônonthiôgoa*, adding *C'est le Roy* [It is the king].

25. Raymond's words here are *Ils sont tous figurés et parabolique*[s].

26. Louis de Buade de Frontenac was governor general of New France from 1672 to 1682 and from 1689 to 1698; Louis-Hector de Callières from 1698 to 1703; and Philippe de Rigaud de Vaudreuil from 1703 to 1725.

27. Wampum (*porcelaine, pourcelaine, pourceline*), beads or disks originally made from mollusk shells, was highly prized by the Eastern Woodlands and Plains Indians. Strings (branches) and necklaces or belts (*colliers*) of wampum were used as money, ornamentation, archives (as indicated by Raymond), and as important ceremonial adjuncts. They were replaced by small cylinders of glass mixed with pewter or lead imported from Europe. European glass beads traded by the French were called *rassades* or *grains de rassade*; tubular beads used as imitation wampum were called *canons*. (Trudel, *Initiation à la Nouvelle-France*, 34; Gregory A. Waselkov, "French Colonial Trade in the Upper Creek Country," in *Calumet & Fleur-de-Lys*, ed. John A. Walthall and Thomas E. Emerson, [Washington, D.C.: Smithsonian Institution, 1992], 48; McDermott, *A Glossary of Mississippi Valley French*, 126, 133.)

28. The problem identified here by Raymond was one of long standing. For example, Olivier Morel de La Durantaye, the highly respected first commandant of Michilimackinac from 1683 to 1690, submitted a lengthy and detailed bill for his "expenditures in the Ottawa country for the king's service and the execution of the orders of General de la Barre in the years 1683-1684," Archives nationales (Paris), Colonies (hereafter cited as AN Col.) C^{11}A 6:451. This statement in the amount of 2,240 sols for his first year alone, virtually all of it for gifts to the allied

Indians, was approved by New France's Intendant Jacques de Meulles in 1685 but apparently rejected by the minister. (This statement is transcribed in the *Bulletin des recherches historiques* (hereafter cited as *BRH*) Lévis, Québec, 1948, 30:49-51. Its translation is in Theodore Calvin Pease and Ernestine Jenison, editors, *Collections of the Illinois State Library* (hereafter cited as *IHC*), 38 vols. (Springfield: Illinois State Historical Library, 1903-75), 23:60-67.

Upon La Durantaye's appeals to Louis XIV, the king in 1700 finally issued instructions to the governor general and intendant, conveyed by the minister as follows: "His Majesty was not willing to satisfy M. de La Durantaye's claims regarding the supplies he asserts he furnished at Missilimaquinac starting in the year 1683, but he was willing to grant him a total of 1,500 livres for all his claims in this matter, in return for which he no longer wants to hear anything about it. He has had the order given for a gratuity [*gratification*] in order to honor him, although it is solely for this supposed compensation, and that is what you must explain to him." (AN Col., B 22:109 recto-109 verso)

This succession of events may be the precedent for the *gratifications* regularly paid by the government to post commanders who did not have their posts' trade to offset their expenses. These *gratifications* became in effect supplementary pay or allowances for the key officers at such posts. Raymond devotes considerable attention to proposed changes in this system in his *dénombrement*.

29. For a mid-eighteenth-century plan and eyewitness description of Fort Michilimackinac and photographs of its reconstruction, see Marie Gérin-Lajoie, trans. and ed., *Fort Michilimackinac in 1749: Lotbinière's Plan and Description* (Mackinac Island, Mich.: Mackinac Island State Park Commission, 1976), vol. 2, leaflet 5. Lotbinière's plan is reproduced on page 94 and Victor Hogg's reconstruction of Michilimackinac is reproduced on page 96 of this volume.

30. The elevation of the Detroit settlement from the status of post to town would have placed it on the governmental level of New France's only three towns, Quebec, Montreal, and, between the two on the St. Lawrence, Trois-Rivières. Detroit would thus have become the first town outside the lower colony. See note 84 below for more on the colony's towns and governance.

31. Baie Verte is south of Prince Edward Island (Ile Saint-Jean), on Northumberland Strait where New Brunswick and Nova Scotia meet. The French fort there was named Fort Gaspareau [Gasparau, Gaspereau; near Port Elgin, New Brunswick].

32. Raymond is referring here to Fort Lawrence, built by the British at Beaubassin, on the other side of a small river east of the French Fort Beauséjour (near Sackville, New Brunswick) at the northeast end of Chignecto Bay, an extension of the Bay of Fundy (la Baie Française). The French fort was just to the west of the uncertain line separating English- and French-controlled mainland territories, and the English fort was just to the east of that line which today separates the provinces of New Brunswick and Nova Scotia. (See R. Cole Harris, ed., *Historical Atlas of Canada*, 3 vols. [Toronto: University of Toronto Press, 1987], 1:plate 30.)

Surlaville (as well as Raymond) was highly critical of the placement of these two French forts by Pierre-Roch de Saint-Ours, one of the French commandants in Acadia, calling their positions "both ridiculous and useless." It was necessary to supply Fort Beauséjour overland ("over four leagues of road") from Fort Gaspareau on Baie Verte at "exorbitant" cost. Fort Beauséjour fell to the British under Robert Monckton in 1755. See Du Boscq de Beaumont, *Les derniers jours de l'Acadie,* 18-21, for Surlaville's condemnatory comments on Saint-Ours in 1751 referring to this and other instances of what Surlaville considered "unpardonable negligence." Du Boscq de Beaumont's work, which carries the subtitle *Extraits du portefeuille de M. Le Courtois de Surlaville, lieutenant-général des armées du roi, ancien major des troupes de l'Ile Royale, mis en ordre at annotés,* is a valuable source of primary information on the efforts of the French to maintain their presence in Acadia.

33. Raymond wrote here *qui ne font que de naître dans le service,* which means literally "who have just barely been born in the service."

34. *Blé d'Inde* is the term for corn in common usage in New France; *blé de Turquie* was used in France but infrequently used in America. Turkish corn was also known as *maiz* or *maïs* in France. (See McDermott, *A Glossary of Mississippi Valley French,* 24, 96; Randle Cotgrave, *A Dictionarie of the French and English Tongues* [London, 1611; reprint, Columbia: University of South Carolina Press, 1950], "Maiz.")

35. The "original" manuscript copy at the Séminaire de Saint-Sulpice in Paris and the National Archives of Canada transcript read here *marchand;* the *RAPQ* transcript reads *marchandises,* correcting either Raymond or the copyist's error.

36. The English post of Choueguen was built on the southern shore of Lake Ontario in 1724. See W. J. Eccles, *France in America,* rev. ed. (East Lansing: Michigan State University Press, 1990), 116, for a succinct statement on the impact of the Oswego contraband trade on the French, and 110-11, 154, and 185 for the importance of Albany in the illegal fur trade.

37. Raymond's use of "you" in this paragraph refers to himself, not Surlaville. As for the remainder of this paragraph, while it is true that in 1754 Raymond received from Louis XV the coveted distinction of being made a *chevalier* of the Royal and Military Order of Saint Louis, the highest recognition possible for a Canadian officer, the honor did nothing to enhance the new *chevalier's* remuneration.

38. The Vermilion River (the Vermilion of the Illinois) flows from the southeast into the Illinois River just west of Starved Rock. Raymond is referring here and in the following paragraph to the Huron Conspiracy of 1747. See note 22 above, for references on this general revolt and its aftermath, which lasted until Charles-Michel Mouet de Langlade's attack on Pickawillany in 1752.

39. La Cloche is situated on the north shore of the North Channel of Georgian Bay. It was on the route from Montreal to the west via the Ottawa River. The location was named after "a rock standing on a plain, which, being struck, rings like a bell," according to Alexander Henry (David A. Armour, ed., *Attack at Michilimackinac: Alexander Henry's Travels and Adventures in Canada and the Indian*

Territories between the years 1760 and 1764 [Mackinac Island: Mackinac Island State Park Commission, 1971], 19).

40. A *chaudière* refers to "rapids that bubble and boil as water does in a kettle" (McDermott, *A Glossary of Mississippi Valley French*, 49). The word basically meant "kettle" in upper country usage. The location Raymond had in mind here is not certain; he may be referring to the *chaudière* situated in the Ottawa River at present-day Ottawa, or to the Chaudière River, flowing northward into the Saint Lawrence River at Quebec. It is very possible that the *chaudière* he was referring to was in the upper country, as are all the other locations in this paragraph.

41. Ile Perrot is off the southwest end of Montreal Island between the Lac des Deux Montagnes and Lac Saint-Louis.

42. Cedars is located about thirty miles upstream from Montreal on the north bank of the St. Lawrence, opposite Valleyfield, beyond the confluence of the Ottawa River.

43. In the summer of 1747 the Ottawas of Saginaw killed three Frenchmen on their way from Detroit to Michilimackinac; two French canoes were attacked by the Chippewa near La Cloche on Georgian Bay, only one of which escaped to Michilimackinac, without its cargo, and the other, containing 8 men, was captured; and another Frenchman was stabbed by the Chippewa just north of Mackinac Island. It was not until 10 August that the first reinforcements of 20 men in 2 canoes led by 2 cadets arrived at Michilimackinac from Montreal. These were followed by a strong detachment of over 75 Frenchmen, mostly militiamen, and 8 Indians under the command of Jacques Legardeur de Saint-Pierre, together with 30,000 pounds of food, ammunition, and supplies. This 10-canoe convoy arrived at Michilimackinac before mid-October, bringing the garrison strength to 100 men. As Raymond stated, this show of strength turned the situation around in the region. For more details on these events, see *Collections of the State Historical Society of Wisconsin* (hereafter cited as *WHC*), 20 vols. (Madison: Society, 1854–1911), 17:462–69 and Peyser, *Jacques Legardeur de Saint-Pierre*, 91–104, 106–11.

44. Although the Tuscaroras moved into Iroquois land early in the eighteenth century, they were "never an equal voting member of the [Iroquois] Confederacy. . . . [T]heir presence gave rise to an impression among Europeans that a sixth nation had been added. The use of the term Six Nations was largely limited to the English and came about gradually, not becoming a common reference until about the time of the American revolution" (Arthur Einhorn, "Six Nations Confederacy," *DCB*, 3:xli).

45. Literally, the Little Rapids, situated at the mouth of Lake Erie, under the Peace Bridge, where the city of Buffalo, New York, now stands. The river at the Petit Rapide location is over 625 meters wide, apparently too wide to be controlled by musket shot, and the width of the Niagara River at Fort Niagara is over 575 meters. The river at Fort Niagara is navigable all the way across, but the rapids at the Petit Rapide may have required passing bateaux and canoes to follow a channel

within musket range of the riverbank (telephone conversation with Brian Leigh Dunnigan, 18 December 1996).

Throughout his report to Surlaville, Raymond pressed for the construction of a French post at this location. In 1758, Governor General Pierre de Rigaud de Vaudreuil-Cavagnial, with the approval of the Iroquois, ordered Daniel-Marie Chabert de Joncaire to establish a post at the Petit Rapide, on the east side of the Niagara River. Under Chabert a number of buildings were constructed and land was cultivated. When Fort Niagara and the surrounding area fell to the British in 1759, the post was destroyed. In 1764, after the Conquest, the British erected Fort Erie on the west side of the Niagara River opposite the Little Rapids. ("Buffalo," The *Encyclopedia Americana*, 30 vols. [New York: Americana Corporation, 1954], 4:691; Daniel de Joncaire-Chabert, *Mémoire pour Daniel de la Joncaire-Chabert, ci-devant commandant au petit Fort de Niagara contre M. le procureur-général de la commission établie pour l'affaire du Canada*, 3 parts in 1 vol. [Paris: Imprimerie de Grange, ca. 1763], part 3:4, 8, 16, 22.)

46. Raymond's use of *qui* here is with the sense of *quiconque*, "anyone." Raymond is inconsistent in his use of *on*, *vous*, and *nous* as indefinite pronoun subjects. All three are indiscriminately used in this *mémoire*. For example, in this paragraph (NAC 2916-17), in the passage beginning with the phrase *Si nous faisions sauter Chöaguin et que vous puissiez vous y maintenir . . .* and ending with the phrase *Chasser les anglois de chöaguin et de la belle riviere . . .* , Raymond uses all three.

47. Raymond's carrot-and-stick plan to force the French-allied Indians to chase the English from Oswego by discontinuing trade in the upper country and requiring the allied Indians to go down to Montreal to trade, while promising to restore the upper country trade if they did force the English out, had several potential major drawbacks. Previously French officials were never able to put a stop to hundreds of coureurs de bois illegally continuing their trade in the woods; indeed, many officers and merchants participated in that illegal trade. It would have been unlikely that officials would be able to stop such trade in the mid-eighteenth century.

Likewise, the French post commanders were not able to stop large-scale contraband trade with the English by their own Indians, as Raymond himself admitted; it is questionable as to how effective the French could be in this. Further, if the French were to have opened fire on their own allies at the strategic passages, as Raymond implied, in addition to having withdrawn their traders from the upper country, how long would it have been before a new general uprising against the French took place? The lesson Gen. Jeffery Amherst learned in 1763 from Pontiac would have surely been taught to Raymond and his superiors, and one would think that Raymond himself would have been less sanguine about his plan in light of his own alarming experience at the Miami post only four years earlier.

Finally, Raymond's proposal to cut off the flow of goods to the Illinois country did not appear to take into consideration the substantial trade between New Orleans and Upper Louisiana (i.e., the Illinois country). Such an attempt would certainly have been opposed by the Louisiana colony officials, who in fact answered to the minister of Marine and the king and not to the governor general of New France.

48. Roland-Michel Barrin de La Galissonière served as commandant general of New France from 1747 to 1749 in the absence of Governor General designate Jacques-Pierre de Taffanel de La Jonquière, who had been captured by the English on his way to Canada.

49. Jean-Victor Varin de La Marre was commissary and controller of the Marine in Quebec and subdelegate of the intendant of New France in Montreal. He held high offices in Canada from 1729 to 1757. Dishonest in the performance of his duties, he was arrested, found guilty, and exiled in connection with the *affaire du Canada* (André Lachance, "Varin de La Marre, Jean-Victor," *DCB*, 4:749-50). The officer who replaced Raymond as commandant at Niagara in 1749 was the distinguished Daniel-Hyacinthe Liénard de Beaujeu (Malcolm MacLeod, "Liénard de Beaujeu, Daniel-Hyacinthe-Marie," *DCB*, 3:400-1).

50. Fort Little Niagara was constructed in 1751 by Daniel-Marie Chabert de Joncaire about one and a half miles above the falls (Walter S. Dunn Jr., "Chabert de Joncaire de Clausonne, Daniel-Marie," *DCB*, 4:137; de Joncaire-Chabert, *Mémoire pour Daniel de la Joncaire-Chabert*, part 1:10-11).

51. The following passage presents various problems for the reader. The "original" of Raymond's *dénombrement* in the archives of the Séminaire de Saint-Sulpice in Paris, which is actually a copy done by a scribe undoubtedly for Surlaville, contains an omission and/or other error after *a son compte et profit*, on folio 144 verso. The NAC transcript (2919) accurately reproduces this folio with the error or errors, whereas Fauteux's *RAPQ* transcript (331) compounds the error by omitting the *de* after *profit*. The passage in question, part of which is consequently not clear, is as follows, as originally written:

> *a quoy sert donc ce fort? il sert a ceux que le Roy paye et nourrit et y entretient pour y faire le commerce qu'on dit que Sa majesté ordonnent de faire a son compte et profit de le faire pour Eux d'envoyer a montreal par les voyageurs qui descendent du detroit les pelletries quil y font a montreal; et le Castor quils font; ils le font porter a Chöaguin par des Sauvages a leurs devotion pour lequel ils font venir du drap anglais des indiennes et autres marchandises prohibées quils vendent a ces memes voyageurs. . . .*

The key to this problem appears to lie in the pronoun *y* (meaning "there") in the phrase *les pelletries quil y font*; it probably refers to Detroit and not Montreal; the following *a Montreal* means "to Montreal" and not "at Montreal," as Surlaville appears to have believed (see below). The voyageurs coming down from Detroit obtain their furs there and take them down to Montreal from Detroit, but the beaver they obtain at Detroit is sent to the English by the king's traders at Niagara using Indian accomplices.

The difficulty in understanding and translating this defective passage is compounded by unclear antecedents for various third-person pronoun subjects and objects. Even Surlaville (NAC 3008-9) seems to have misunderstood this passage by rewriting it in such a way that the king's men at the little Niagara fort "are sending to Oswego and the other English posts by voyageurs and even trusted Indians *the furs and beaver that come to them from Montreal via Detroit* [emphasis added], and are having prohibited goods brought back from the English that they then sell to these same voyageurs when they go back up to Detroit":

> *Ce fort ne sert précisément qu'à ceux que le Roy paye et Nourrit pour le garder, ils y font à leur Compte un commerce que le Roy s'était réservé pour le sien. ils Envoyent par des Voyageurs et par des Sauvages mêmes affidés à Chouaguin, et aux autres postes anglois, les pelletries et Castors qui leur arrivent de Montreal par le Détroit; et font revenir de chez L'anglois des Marchandises prohibées qu'ils vendent Ensuite à ces mêmes Voyageurs lorsqu'ils remontent le Détroit.*

The present translation of Raymond's passage is an interpretive effort to tie logically all the elements into a cohesive whole, using bracketed clarifications to render it more comprehensible.

While Raymond does not identify by name the "king's traders" at Little Fort Niagara, Daniel Chabert de Joncaire commanded that fort from 1751 to its destruction in 1759 and held the trade monopoly of the portage. After the Conquest, he was first imprisoned in the Bastille, then tried and convicted for irregularities in his record keeping, and finally released with only a warning (Dunn, "Chabert de Joncaire," *DCB*, 4:137-38).

52. See note 45 above.

53. This river is located "just above Niagara Falls on the west bank of the Niagara River" (Cardy, trans., and Dunnigan, ed., *Memoirs on the Late War in North America*, 194n. 587).

54. *La petite guerre* can also be translated as "guerilla warfare," but perhaps "hit-and-run" would better describe the nature of the hostilities in the Ohio Valley at this point in time (late 1754). See W. J. Eccles's descriptions of this type of warfare in *France in America*: "In Canada the war became one of guerilla tactics, what the French call *la petite guerre*. . . . Most of the fighting was done by the Canadian militia in small war parties led by regular [colonial] officers, many of them Canadian. . . . [T]hey mastered the techniques of this savage forest warfare of swift raid and ambush. . . ." (103); ". . . the civilian militia bore the brunt of the fighting in the *petite guerre*" (123). In his "The French Forces in North America during the Seven Years' War," Eccles wrote that the *Troupes de la Marine* "had had to master the art of guerilla fighting both against and alongside the Indian nations," *DCB*, 3:xvii. The Canadian mastery of guerilla fighting reached a high point in

1755 with Daniel-Hyacinthe-Marie Liénard de Beaujeu and Jean-Daniel Dumas leading a detachment of 637 Indians, 146 Canadian militiamen, and only 108 officers and men of the *Troupes de la Marine* in their great victory over Edward Braddock's powerful army near Fort Duquesne (MacLeod, "Liénard de Beaujeu," *DCB*, 3:401-2).

55. The NAC transcript incorrectly states 570 leagues; Fauteux correctly transcribed the number as 170. *Engagés* were employees of the fur trade.

56. McDermott, *A Glossary of Mississippi Valley French*, 20, describes a *barque* as a boat with a capacity of 45 to 50 tons, equipped with mast and sails as well as oars, the latter for use on rivers.

57. See note 18 above, on bat(t)eaux.

58. The meaning of the term *batteaux du cent*, written *batteaux de cent* later on by Raymond, and *bateaux du cens* by Surlaville, is not entirely clear. Peter W. Halford, *Le français des Canadiens à la veille de la Conquête: Témoignage du père Pierre Philippe Potier, s.j.* (Ottawa: Les Presses de l'université d'Ottawa, 1994), 236, speculates that a *bateau du cent* could have meant a large canoe capable of carrying 100 (*cent*) packs of furs. He also cites Alexander Henry, *Travels and Adventures in Canada and the Indian Territories between the Years 1760 and 1776* (New York, 1809; facsimile reprint, Ann Arbor: University Microfilms, 1966), 184, who wrote of barges on Lake Erie around 1760, "capable of carrying a hundred men each, with their provisions."

The context in which the term is used in Raymond's *mémoire* establishes the primary purpose of these *batteaux du cent* as carrying freight. This is confirmed by Raymond near the end of this document, on folio 168 verso (NAC 2978), where he describes these boats under the heading *Barques* (barks), each carrying six to eight thousand pounds of weight. On page 146 verso (NAC 2924) he states that barks are used for carrying freight. Barques are small boats with or without decks (*Grand Larousse en 5 volumes*, [Paris: 1987], 1:309) and with a mast and sails (McDermott, *A Glossary of Mississippi Valley French*, 20). On folio 156 verso (NAC 2949), Raymond appears to differentiate between barks and *batteaux du cent*, both of which are used for transporting freight.

59. The legs or stages by water of Raymond's proposed transshipments can be summarized as follows: The furs would be

1. brought from the upper country by canoe to the Petit Rapide, then
2. taken by bark from the Petit Rapide to the head of the Niagara portage; then
3. taken by bateau from the lower end of the portage to Fort Niagara; and then
4. taken by bark from Fort Niagara to Fort Frontenac; then
5. taken from Fort Frontenac by *batteaux du cent* to Montreal.

Raymond does not mention here the cartage necessary to transport the furs from Lachine to Montreal. He does describe this cartage below (folio 168v; NAC 2978-79).

60. See notes 31 and 32 above, for the locations of Baie Verte and Fort Beauséjour. Chibouctou (Chibucto) Harbor is on the Atlantic coast of Nova Scotia and is the site of Halifax, founded there by the British in 1749. Mirliguèche was on the coast fewer than 50 miles southwest of Halifax, near today's Lunenburg.

61. Lake Megantic, Quebec, is about one hundred miles south of Quebec City, near the Maine border. The Chaudière River flows northward from the lake into the St. Lawrence River at Quebec, near the present Quebec bridge. The Chaudière falls are located near the mouth of the river.

    I am indebted to Pauleena MacDougall of the Maine Folklore Center of the University of Maine in Orono for her kind assistance in providing information on several places named by Raymond in this section. The English fort constructed in 1754 below Naransouack (probably Norridgewock, Maine) evidently was Fort Halifax at Winslow (Taconic Falls), Maine. Fort Western was built the same year at Augusta, some 20 miles to the south. The fort at Naransouak village reported by "the first Abenaki who had come from that direction" may have been the English fort which stood at Norridgewock in 1704-5.

    The portage mentioned by Raymond may be Northeast Carry, which is only 2 or 3 miles, not 4 leagues (10 miles). Northeast Carry connects Moosehead Lake with the West Branch of the Penobscot River. The Moose River flows between Moosehead Lake and the Maine-Quebec-border area, from which a portage could link the Moose River to the Chaudière River. Sasagues8anaudin remains unidentified. The initial, reduplicated form in this word, *sasag-*, comes from the root *sah-* meaning upright. The latter part of this word means at a promontory, or point of land and mountain (*kwesso* = promontory, cliff; *aten* = mountain), which may describe Mt. Kineo, shiny cliffs of rhyolite along Moosehead Lake. Letters from Pauleena MacDougall to the author, 9 and 20 December 1996.

    For details on the Anglo-Abenaki wars and the French and Indian War in Acadia, see David L. Ghere, "Diplomacy & War on the Maine Frontier, 1678-1759, in *Maine: The Pine Tree State from Prehistory to the Present*, ed. Richard W. Judd, Edwin A. Churchill, and Joel W. Eastman (Orono: University of Maine Press, 1995), 120-42.

62. Beauce is a region of Quebec extending to the Maine border southeast of Quebec City through which the Chaudière River flows.

63. Governor General Frontenac and Intendant Champigny paid a bounty to their French-allied Iroquois of 10 écus, equivalent to 30 livres, for each English-allied Iroquois enemy scalp during King William's War (1689-97), the North American phase of the War of the Grand Alliance. See Peyser, *Letters from New France*, 58-59, for additional details on this practice. Raymond's recommendation here, however, crosses a racial dividing line, in that this time he would have the French pay for English scalps.

64. Some members of the families named here by Raymond include Claude de Ramezay, governor of Montreal and acting governor of New France from 1714

to 1716, whose son Jean-Baptiste-Nicolas-Roch de Ramezay commanded several posts in the 1730s and 1740s; two sons of Jean-Louis de La Corne, founder of one of the most important families in New France, who each served at Michilimackinac, Louis as commander in 1745-47 and François-Josué as second in command in 1733-39; Paul Marin de La Malgue, an officer and son of a distinguished but commoner soldier, who took command of Chagouamigon (Ashland, Wisconsin) in 1722 and commanded Green Bay in 1748-53, and whose son, Joseph, succeeded his father as commander of those two posts; the highly placed Pierre Legardeur de Repentigny, who had arrived in New France in 1636 and had two of his grandsons command Michilimackinac: Jean-Baptiste-René in 1733, when he was killed in action against the Foxes, and the noted Jacques Legardeur de Saint-Pierre in 1747-49; Nicolas-Antoine Coulon de Villiers, hero of the Fox Wars, who with his sons and son-in-law commanded the St. Joseph, Green Bay, and Miami posts; Louis Liénard de Beaujeu, who commanded Michilimackinac from 1719 to 1722, and who had two illustrious sons, Daniel-Hyacinthe, who died leading his men against Braddock in 1755, and Louis, the last commander of Michilimackinac (1757-60) before the Conquest; Jacques-Pierre Daneau de Muy, commander of Fort St. Joseph (1731-35), Fort Chambly (1752-54), and Detroit (1754-58), the son of Nicolas Daneau de Muy, governor-designate of Louisiana in 1707-8.

The other families named by Raymond include the Céloron de Blainville brothers, Jean-Baptiste and the noted Pierre-Joseph, who successively commanded Michilimackinac from 1736 to 1742 in addition to their subsequent commands at Fort St. Joseph (Niles, Michigan), Niagara, Fort Saint Frédéric (Crown Point, New York), and Detroit; the Boucher de La Perrière men, members of an illustrious military family, who commanded a number of the forts ranging from Fort Beauharnois among the Sioux (René in 1727-28) to Fort Saint-Frédéric (René in 1732-33) and Niagara (François-Clément in 1754-55); and Jacques-Hugues Péan de Livaudière, who commanded Forts Frontenac (Kingston, Ontario, 1722-25), Chambly (south of Montreal, 1727-29), and Detroit (1734), and whose son, Michel-Jean-Hugues Péan, also an officer in the *Troupes de la Marine*, became a millionaire through his unscrupulous association with Intendant François Bigot in fraudulently supplying the upper country forts and in the trade of the colony.

François-Marc-Antoine Le Mercier, also known as Mercier, was an artillery officer and engineer active during the 1740s and 1750s in the French campaigns in Acadia, the New York frontier region, and the Ohio Valley, but not a fort commander. In 1753 and 1754 he built Forts Presqu'Ile, Rivière aux boeufs, and Duquesne (Jean Pariseau, "Le Mercier [Mercier], François-Marc-Antoine," *DCB*, 4:459). Louis-Antoine de Bougainville, Louis-Joseph de Montcalm's aide-de-camp, referred in 1757 to Captain Le Mercier's "talent for enriching himself, a talent too common in this country to merit attaching any importance to" (*BRH*, 37:456).

Raymond's statement that "The first has La Pointe with St. Luc La Corne and half of many other posts" (or "the first at La Pointe with St. Luc La Corne . . . ," depending on whether the word has a grave accent or not) is unclear. Luc de La Corne, also known as La Corne Saint-Luc and Saint-Luc La Corne, did indeed have the trading rights as a major partner at many of the frontier posts, including the one at La Pointe (Chagouamigon) from 1752 to 1755. La Corne Saint-Luc's written partnership, however, was with Louis-Joseph Gaultier de La Vérendrye, the post's commandant (Pierre Tousignant and Madeleine Dionne-Tousignant, "La Corne, Luc de," *DCB*, 4:425), and not with a Ramezay (the first listed family name) as inferred by Raymond's reference to "the first . . . with St. Luc La Corne." It should be noted, nonetheless, that Jean-Baptiste-Nicolas-Roch de Ramezay, Claude de Ramezay's son, did command Chagouamigon from 1731 to 1733.

Raymond's use here of "the whole Illinois River" as a comprehensive term to include all of the Canadian posts under the command of the families he lists is misleading. The Illinois country was part of Upper Louisiana, since 1717 under the jurisdiction of the governor of Louisiana and not the governor general of New France (Canada). The posts and settlements on the Illinois River were not part of Canada, then, nor was the Vincennes post on the Wabash River; their commandants were named by the Louisiana authorities.

65. The problem of inadequate salaries identified here by Raymond extended, of course, to married officers, placing them in desperate straits throughout the history of New France. For example, in 1686 Governor General Jacques-René Brisay de Denonville reported several respected officers' families "who are reduced to begging." One of the officers asked "for permission to withdraw to France in order to seek the wherewithal to survive and to place his children in service in the homes of those who will be willing to feed them" (NAC: MG5, B1, vol. 5, part 3: transcript pp. 391-92).

In 1737, Governor General Charles de Beauharnois and Intendant Gilles Hocquart reported the plight of Marie de La Porte de Louvigny, widow of Captain Jacques Testard de Montigny, whose last assignment was as commander of Michilimackinac. The officials reported to the minister that the officer's widow, "burdened with five daughters and a boy of 15 or 16 years beseeches us to make known to you the sad position to which she finds herself and her family reduced, having no possessions for raising it other than a house in Montreal." They entreated the minister for "a pension which might be able to help her live with her family" (Archives du Séminaire de Québec, article CR-1941-271).

Compounding the already serious problem of the officers' inadequate and fixed pay was the rampant inflation that characterized Intendant François Bigot's administration (1748-60). Some examples of this inflation, due to a variety of causes including Bigot's malversation, illustrate the problem from January 1751 to January 1755: the price of a pound of beef or bacon increased by 67 percent; a dozen eggs rose by

233 percent; milk by 166 percent; a pair of wool stockings by 133 percent; a shirt by 60 percent. By 1759, the prices had risen more than tenfold for meat, and for items of clothing, as much as 300 to 700 percent (Commissaire des Guerres au Ministre, Québec, le 20 janvier 1759, NAC: MG5, Ministère des Affaires étrangères [Paris], Mémoires et Documents: Amérique, B1, vol. 11, transcript pp. 85-86). See the chart on page 79 graphically showing the growth of inflation in these years.

See part I, note 4 and note 67 below, for information on the unit of money called the livre, and note 79 below for an explanation of the unit of weight also called the livre.

66. The officers' regular salary was called *appointements*, which in 1754 was 1,062 livres a year for a captain. The king upon various occasions approved special payments to officers, called *gratifications*. While one translation of the term can be "bonus," it is better defined here as an amount of money given to someone beyond what is normally due that person, particularly in reference to officers of the *Troupes de la Marine* who commanded certain frontier posts. In the 1740s and 1750s, a *gratification* or supplementary pay of 3,000 livres a year was routinely given to post commanders who did not have the trade at their posts, and lesser amounts to the subordinate officers. The money for this supplementary pay came from the sale of congés to merchants and voyageurs who wished to trade at those posts.

In 1751, 13 of these trade licenses were sold by the governor general for trading at Michilimackinac, producing 7,800 livres of income, from which 4,500 livres for the officers' supplementary pay was taken (AN Col., C¹¹A 119:400-2). Raymond's proposed plan would raise the price of a congé to 1,000 livres, and he would increase the commanders' supplementary pay as he explains in the following paragraphs. It should be noted that in the then-existing system, commanders who had the trade of their posts (with no congés permitted) had to pay for the expenses of the post from the proceeds of their trade.

67. The *écu blanc* or *petit écu* was worth three livres. Under the ancien régime the franc was a coin struck in both gold and silver equivalent to one livre. The livre was a monetary accounting term, used to evaluate the great variety of nonstandardized coins in use. See Trudel, *Initiation à la Nouvelle-France*, 197-201, for a succinct explanation of the disorganized monetary systems of New France and France.

68. Forts Presqu'Ile and Le Boeuf were built in 1753; Fort Duquesne was built in 1754. The year in which this letter was written is therefore 1754. Louis Coulon de Villiers's successful attack against George Washington, mentioned in the next phrase, occurred on 3 July 1754, making the date of this report subsequent to that event.

69. Raymond identified here the four critical posts as Forts Frontenac, Niagara, Detroit, and Michilimackinac.

70. For translations of the minister's letter to Duquesne and of Duquesne's negative response, see part I, pp. 3-4 in this volume.

71. A pistole was an accounting term; it was worth 10 livres. The congés proposed by Raymond would therefore be sold for 1,000 livres.

72. Congés, limited in number, were awarded by the governor general and visaed by the indendant of New France. The exact location where the trading was to be done, the number of canoes and engagés permitted on the expedition, the amount of brandy allowed (for personal consumption only), and the time established for the return to Montreal were all written in the congé. This explains Raymond's repeated references to the "filling out" of congés, which in this translation is rendered henceforth as obtaining, purchasing, or selling congés.

73. The word used by Raymond is *lard*, which in Canadian usage refers to the meat of a pig. In France, *lard* used alone can mean either fat (of a pig) or bacon; *lard maigre* or *petit lard* refer to bacon; *gros lard* or *lard gras* refer to fat (of a pig). In Canada and France, the word *graisse* means animal fat. For the Canadian usage of *lard*, see La Société du parler français au Canada, *Glossaire du parler français au Canada* (Québec: Les Presses de l'Université Laval, 1968), 418.

74. A *pot* consisted of about one-half gallon.

75. A *velte* consisted of about two gallons.

76. A *quart* was a wooden barrel whose capacity was about 27 to 45 gallons. See Nicole Genêt, Luce Vermette, and Louise Décarie-Audet, *Les Objets de nos ancêtres* (Montréal: Les Editions de l'homme, 1974), 215, and Trudel, *Initiation à la Nouvelle-France*, 238.

77. See note 14, above, on the Abbé Picquet.

78. *Un enseigne en pied et un en second d'augmentation.* The full or first ensign (*enseigne en pied*) and the second ensign (*enseigne en second*) under the ancien régime are equivalent to today's *enseigne (de vaisseau) de 1re classe* and *enseigne (de vaisseau) de 2e classe* in the French Navy. These two ranks correspond to today's French Army and French Air Force's ranks of first lieutenant and second lieutenant, respectively (*Grand Larousse en 5 volumes* [Paris: Librairie Larousse, 1987], 2:1098; 3:1423; Paul Robert, *Le Petit Robert: Dictionnaire alphabétique & analogique de la langue française* [Paris: Société du Nouveau Littré, 1978], 651).

79. The word *livre*, of feminine gender, referred not only to the monetary accounting term, but also to the unit of weight (489.41 grams, as compared to the U.S. pound, which weighs 454 grams). The *livre* weight unit in New France was occasionally referred to as a *livre pesant* (pound weight) to distinguish it from the monetary unit. The weight unit is correctly translated as "pound," whereas the monetary unit is left in English as "livre." Raymond wrote here *4,000 pesant*, with the word *livres* understood. See Lester A. Ross, *Archaeological Metrology: English, French, American and Canadian Systems of Weights and Measures for North American Archaeology*, History and Archeology Series, No. 68 (Hull, Canada: Canadian Government Publishing Center, Supply and Services Canada, 1983), 29, 59.

80. The monetary system was as follows: there were 20 sols to a livre, and 12 deniers to a sol. Raymond is therefore recommending here paying one and a half livres

per *pot* of wine. These prices were less than retail prices in the lower colony at this time. For Raymond's listing of food prices in 1754, see NAC pages 2972-77 (original folios 166 recto–168 recto).

81. A *setier, sétier,* or *septier* was, under the ancien régime, a measure of capacity varying according to the region (*Grand Larousse en 5 volumes,* 5:2809). It contained eight *pintes; a pinte de Paris* was equivalent to about one U.S. quart or one liter (Paul Robert, *Dictionnaire alphabétique et analogique de la langue française,* 6 vols. [Paris: Société du Nouveau Littré, 1962], 6:423; Ross, *Archaeological Metrology,* 74). A *setier* in Paris would therefore have been the equivalent of about eight U.S. quarts or two gallons. Raymond's wine ration of one *septier* and a half per day per man would therefore have been, in U.S. measure, three gallons (12 quarts) per day, highly unlikely.

    Under *septier,* Randle Cotgrave's early seventeenth-century *Dictionarie of the French and English Tongues* (London, 1611; reprint, Columbia: University of South Carolina Press, 1950, 1968) lists *septier de vin* as containing eight pints, confirming the above equivalency, but Cotgrave also lists in his article *demi septier de vin,* stating that it "Is but the halfe of a *Chopine,* or a quarter of the French pint." Robert's article on *setier* states that *demi-setier* is used for a quarter of a liter, confirming Cotgrave. (Ross, however, states that a *demi-septier* was about one-third of a *septier*). Applying Cotgrave's equivalency to Raymond's ration of one and one-half *septiers*—which would presumably be three *demi-septiers*—each man would receive three-quarters of a *pinte* (about three-quarters of a U.S. quart, the equivalent of one 750 ml bottle) per day, a far more likely ration. This equivalency is confirmed in Nicole Genêt et al., *Les Objets familiers de nos ancêtres,* 228, which states that a *setier* was equivalent to a *chopine,* that is, half a *pinte,* or a half-liter.

    Under the ancien régime measures were not standardized. The French *pinte* was no exception. Outside Paris, the content of a *pinte* differed substantially from that of the Parisian *pinte* (see Cotgrave, *Dictionarie of the French and English Tongues,* "pinte").

82. Watape (or wattup) was "the small roots of the spruce tree . . . with which the bark is sewed; and the gum of the pine tree supplies the place of tar and oakum." (Armour, ed., *Attack at Michilimackinac,* 7).

83. The original copy and the NAC transcript state *et des marchandises de transport pour la traite,* which illogically transposes the positions of the two terms. The *RAPQ* transcript corrects the copyist's (or Raymond's) error, producing *et de transport des marchandises pour la traite.*

84. The *lieutenant de roi* was an officer ranking below a town governor and above the town major and *aide-major,* all members of the headquarters staff. According to Raymond's recommendations, which were not followed, Detroit would be elevated to the virtual status of a town, with an organizational structure similar to that of Quebec, Montreal, and Trois-Rivières. His proposed placement of a high-ranking king's lieutenant at Michilimackinac would have elevated that key post's

status above all the others (except Detroit), whose commanders were no higher than captain, the highest rank in the *Troupes de la Marine*. See Trudel, *Initiation à la Nouvelle-France*, 167-68, 172 for more on the officers in town administration in New France.

When Raymond wrote this report in 1754, Pierre-Joseph Céloron de Blainville, who had commanded Michilimackinac as a captain in the 1730s and early 1740s, had also served as commandant of the Detroit post with the staff rank of major for three years (to 1753), recognition of that post's importance (and that particular officer's standing). Michilimackinac, however, did not have a commandant above the rank of captain.

85. Raymond's metaphor here is *plus souples qu'un gand* [*gant*], literally, "more supple than a glove."

86. Raymond's motive for writing this lengthy report unequivocally surfaces here.

87. The Paskoya was the name of the Saskatchewan River (Antoine Champagne, *Nouvelles études sur les La Vérendrye et le poste de l'ouest* [Québec: Les Presses de l'Université Laval, 1971], passim; Lawrence J. Burpee, *Journals and Letters of Pierre Gaultier de Varennes de La Vérendrye and His Sons* [Toronto: Champlain Society, 1927], 24, 447n).

88. Masanne was the principal village of the Kickapoo, apparently located to the west of Ouiatanon as described by Nicolas-Joseph de Noyelles de Fleurimont in 1735 (*WHC*, 17:222). Raymond's report indicates that Masanne was near the Illinois River; William B. Brigham and J. Joe Bauxar identified the location of the Grand Kickapoo Village as being about 40 miles east of the Illinois River late in the eighteenth century, in McLean County, Illinois (William B. Brigham, "The Grand Kickapoo Village and Associated Fort in the Illinois Wilderness," *Indian Mounds and Villages*, Bulletin No. 2, Illinois Archeological Survey [Urbana: University of Illinois, 1960], 91-106). Agreeing with Brigham, R. David Edmunds places the Grand Kickapoo Village near Downs in McLean County, Illinois ("A History of the Kickapoo Indians in Illinois from 1750-1834," [master's thesis, Illinois State University, 1966], 13; telephone interview, 22 January 1995). Brigham's article (96) reproduces a portion of René Paul's 1815 map, which shows a second Kickapoo village further west, only about 20 miles from the Illinois River.

89. Fort de Chartres was located on the east bank of the Mississippi River just west of Prairie du Rocher, Illinois. This massive stone fort was the bastion of the upper Louisiana colony. Since 1717 the Illinois country was part of the colony of Louisiana and answered to New Orleans, not Quebec.

90. Missisquoi Bay, lying at the northeast end of Lake Champlain. The northern half of this bay lies in the Province of Quebec, the southern half in Vermont.

91. The Long Saut was the long rapids on the Ottawa River one day west of Montreal where the extensive portage discouraged monitoring beyond it.

92. The village of Kethtippecanunk, inhabited by Miami, possibly Ouiatanon Indians in 1742, was situated upstream (north) on the Tippecanoe River about 25 kilometers

from Fort Ouiatanon (West Lafayette, Indiana). For information on Kethtippecanunk, see Neal L. Trubowitz, "Native Americans and French on the Central Wabash," in Walthall and Emerson, eds., *Calumet & Fleur-de-Lys*, 256-57.

93. Elkhart, Indiana, is some 100 miles northeast of Fort Ouiatanon and about 60 miles northwest of Fort Miami. *Coeur de cerf* literally translated means "stag's (or elk's) heart." "The city took its name from Island Park, which, according to Indian legend, resembles an elk's heart" (*Encyclopedia Americana*, 30 vols. [New York: Americana Corporation, 1954], 10:250).

94. Charles Germain was a highly regarded Jesuit missionary to the Malecite Indians of the Saint John River. He also served as chaplain to the French garrison at Fort Menagouèche (Saint John, New Brunswick). See Micheline D. Johnson, "Germain, Charles," *DCB*, 4:289-90.

95. The Abbé Jean-Louis Le Loutre was missionary and French agent among the Micmac in Acadia. His incitement of the Indians to war against the British resulted in a price being put upon his head. In 1754 he was made vicar general in Acadia. His anti-British activities included paying 1,800 livres for 18 British scalps taken in raids by the Micmacs. Upon the fall of Fort Beauséjour, he left New France, only to be taken prisoner when his ship was captured by the British in September 1755. He was released only after the signing of the Treaty of Paris of 1763 (Gérard Finn, "Le Loutre, Jean-Louis," *DCB*, 4:453-58 passim).

96. Charles-François-Xavier Tarieu de La Pérade, son of the great heroine of New France, Madeleine de Verchères, commanded the Miami post until 1741. His successor there, Jacques Legardeur de Saint-Pierre, reported that La Pérade had permitted smugglers to pass through the post. La Pérade was commander of the Ouiatanon post in 1747. The brothers Legardeur de Repentigny, Pierre and Louis, often mistaken for one another, were the sons of Jean-Baptiste Legardeur de Repentigny, who commanded Michilimackinac in 1733. The elder of the two, Pierre, commanded Fort St. Joseph in 1750; Louis, known as the Chevalier de Repentigny, was second-in-command at Michilimackinac in 1748 and commander of Sault-Saint-Louis from 1750 to around 1758. Jacques Legardeur de Saint-Pierre is known to have traded heavily in brandy as commander of the Western Sea posts (mainly in Manitoba, Canada) from 1750 to 1753. Louis de La Corne, the older brother of La Corne Saint-Luc, known as the Chevalier de La Corne, succeeded Saint-Pierre as commander of the Western Sea posts from 1753 to 1755.

97. A *cas réservé* is a sin that only the bishop or pope can absolve.

98. The original copy in the Archives du Séminaire de Saint-Sulpice in Paris has errors in this sentence (on folio 160 verso) that were made, in all probability, by both Raymond and the eighteenth-century copyist. The National Archives of Canada and *Rapport de l'Archiviste de la Province de Québec* transcripts of the sentence differ, and the syntax in both versions is incorrect. Page 2958 of the NAC transcript records the sentence as *l'interêt est a la cause de Dieu ne doit avoir acception*

de personne, whereas the transcript printed on page 345 of the 1927-28 *RAPQ* reads as follows: *L'intérêt et la cause de Dieu ne doit avoir acception de personne.*

Upon reading the original in Paris in 1994, I found that two words (or fragments) were crossed out here (by the copyist) and one word (*et*) was written in by him, leaving a certain lack of clarity. I found the sentence as follows: *l'interêts* [*sic*] *et la cause de Dieu ne doit* [*sic*] *avoir acception de personne*; my analysis of the problems in the sentence follows.

The word *acception* is not a misspelling of *exception*. Paul Robert, *Dictionnaire alphabétique et analogique de la langue française*, 6 vols. (Paris: Société du Nouveau Littré, 1960), 1:25, provides an explicit explanation of *acception*: *Action de considérer la qualité d'une personne au préjudice d'une autre personne.* The context of Raymond's argument confirms his use of *acception* here.

The meaning of the word *intérêt* is ambiguous in this sentence. Do the words "interest" and "God's cause" as used by Raymond here mean "God's interest and cause," or did Raymond have in mind for *intérêt* the general interest here? It is unlikely that there is an unequivocal answer. Surlaville's papers contain another version of sections of Raymond's report (transcribed in Du Boscq de Beaumont, *Les derniers jours de l'Acadie*, 281) in which Raymond presented his same argument about the brandy trade. In this version he wrote "Qu'on laisse donc, au sujet du commerce d'eau-de-vie, l'entière liberté de conscience; le fasse qui voudra et ne le fasse pas celui que cela répugnera. Si on persiste dans cette défense, *il faut qu'elle soit pour tout le monde en général*, qu'il n'y ait personne de privilégié, comme il y en a, et pendre le premier qui en vendra" [italics mine].

This sentence may provide further insight into Raymond's thinking: "Let them allow, then, concerning the brandy trade, complete freedom of conscience; let it be done by those who want to and let those who are repelled by it not do it. If they persist in that prohibition, *it is necessary that it be for everyone in general*, that there be no favorites, as there are, and [it is necessary to] hang the first person to sell any." In Raymond's eyes, it would appear that the general interest (including his own) is at stake at least as much as God's cause.

99. The 17 captains include the 6 at Detroit plus the 11 commandants at the other posts listed above Detroit.

100. Raymond wrote here *presqu'en partie*, "almost partially," undoubtedly meaning to write *presqu'entièrement*, "almost entirely."

101. See above folio 135 verso (NAC 2897) for Raymond's earlier remarks on this post.

102. See note 19 above, for details on this Sulpician mission.

103. The *Saut* (The Falls) refers here to Le Sault St.-Louis (Caughnawaga or Kahnawake, Quebec), where the Jesuits had a mission east of the Sulpician mission at the Lac des Deux Montagnes (Oka, Quebec).

104. Raymond provides here several illustrations of the French accommodating to the Indians and meeting with them on the "middle ground." See Richard White, *The*

Middle Ground: Indians, Empires, and Republics in the Great Lakes Region, 1650-1815 (Cambridge: Cambridge University Press, 1991).

105. It was the regular practice of Intendant François Bigot to reduce the amounts specified on most of the certificates or vouchers when they were presented for payment in Quebec. His own large-scale embezzlements did not prevent him from attempting to reduce the illicit profits made by post commanders and others not part of his own clique.

106. *Les bourgeois négotians* [sic]. See McDermott, *A Glossary of Mississippi Valley French*, 34, for a description of this fur-trade term used here by Raymond.

107. Many of these partnerships, called *sociétés*, were legal, others were not. The worst offenders were in Bigot's *Grande Société*, defined by J. F. Bosher and J.-C. Dubé as "a system of private enterprise on a grand scale with the collaboration of most of the other colonial officials and many army officers and merchants working under the terms of personal understandings or even formal companies" (Bosher and Dubé, "Bigot, François," *DCB*, 4:65). See Gratien Allaire, "Officiers et marchands: Les Sociétés de commerce des fourrures, 1715-1760," *Revue d'histoire de l'Amérique française* 40, no. 3 (winter 1987): 409-27 for a well-documented analysis of the fur-trade partnerships involving post commanders, officers, and *marchands-voyageurs*.

108. The original manuscript has *castonnade* here, a misspelling of *cassonade*, sugar that has been refined only once.

109. In 1720, a similar position was created for the distinguished officer of the *Troupes de la Marine* Louis de La Porte de Louvigny. The high cost of the anticipated inspection tours of the upper country posts prevented their actually being carried out. See Yves F. Zoltvany, "La Porte de Louvigny, Louis de," *DCB*, 2:346, for additional details on Louvigny's special appointment as "commander-in-chief of the pays d'en haut."

110. *Affermé*, "farmed out," means "leased out," usually to a civilian merchant. There were instances in which military commanders who were "given" the trading post at their fort leased it, for their own profit, as Raymond wrote, to civilians. The English translation of an interesting and informative contract for such an arrangement in 1735 between Lieutenant Philippe Damour de La Morandière, commandant at the Miami post, and Thérèse Catin and her husband is in Joseph L. Peyser, "The Fall and Rise of Thérèse Catin: A Portrait from Indiana's French and Canadian History," *Indiana Magazine of History* 91, no. 4 (December 1995): 378-79.

111. Raymond wrote here, *Tout ce qui ne sort point de la minerve de ceux à qui on s'en raporte* [sic] *n'est jamais aprouvé* [sic]. *On vous fait passer pour un imposteur.*

IV. COMPARATIVE ANALYSIS OF RAYMOND'S AND SURLAVILLE'S REPORTS

For the reader who wishes systematically to compare the content of Surlaville's report with that of Raymond's enumeration (see pages 30-32 for the topical outline of the latter's *dénombrement*), a topical outline of Surlaville's *mémoire* is provided in appendix 1.

The most obvious differences between Raymond's and Surlaville's *mémoires* are the disparities in length (Surlaville's is shorter by one-third) and the significant omissions made by Surlaville. The higher level of Surlaville's spelling and written expression, and his use of shorter paragraphs than Raymond's (which occasionally run on for three large folio pages) are readily distinguishable differences.

Less obvious is the difference in the organization of the content by the two men; Surlaville attempted, generally successfully, to group together material on the same topic. For example, he wrote but one section, under the bold heading "Character of the Indians," on the nature and customs of the Indians (on NAC transcript pages 3017-22); Raymond, on the other hand, had placed this content under inappropriate headings in different locations in his report (NAC 2901-5 and 2967-68). Many of Raymond's digressions are under headings unrelated to them, whereas this tendency is virtually eliminated in the Surlaville manuscript.

Like Raymond, Surlaville introduced his report with a three-paragraph summation of the points he was going to cover, calling his report, in part, a *Mémoire en forme d'observations*. Raymond did not head his *mémoire* with a title, but he referred to it in his first paragraph by the underlined words *le dénombrement de tous les postes du Canada*. Raymond divided his *dénombrement* into three major sections, each of which he headed by a bold Roman numeral. In the body of his report, Raymond used bold lettering merely to begin each paragraph, not to indicate a subhead. He did use bold, centered

141

First page of Colonel Michel Le Courtois de Surlaville's *Mémoire en forme d'observations concernant le dénombrement des postes du Canada . . .*, 1754. Reproduced with permission of the Archives de Saint-Sulpice, Paris, from manuscrit 1200, pièce 38 of the collection "Pièces pour l'histoire militaire du Canada 1730-1760."

subheads on occasion, but in an inconsistent manner. Consequently, the organization of his report is not readily discernible to the reader.

Unlike Raymond, Surlaville clearly marked his report's divisions and subdivisions with large, centered bold heads and subheads, reflecting in part the better organization of this document. Obviously, Surlaville's heavily edited administrative version is the more readable and accessible of the two, but it lacks most of the color and human quality, and all of the vitriol, found in Raymond's *dénombrement*. Surlaville possessed "a literary ability far beyond most of his contemporaries,"[1] which is particularly evident in comparing his report to the one written by a colonial officer who spent most of his life on the frontier. Yet the latter manuscript makes far more interesting and lively reading.

It is instructive to examine a number of the points that Surlaville deleted, modified, and retained in his *mémoire* vis-à-vis Raymond's *dénombrement*. As previously mentioned, the latter's frequent carping and references to his own perceived plight were omitted in Surlaville's report. Likewise omitted were any mention of Raymond's offers to carry out his proposed plan as major in command of Michilimackinac or with the concession of Green Bay as a seigniory (both on NAC 2951), or as inspector general of the troops, garrisons and posts of the upper country (NAC 2981).

In editing the *dénombrement* for presentation to the minister, Surlaville took care to avoid involvement in the long-standing tension between church and state over the brandy trade, even though in his report Raymond had tempered the antipathy he felt toward the Jesuits, "Messrs. the casuists of Canada," that he expressed in another letter to his friend.[2] Raymond's long digression (NAC 2954-58) promoting the open sale of brandy to the Indians at all the French posts—containing his criticisms of the "ecclesiastical power [in New France] and the country's government," and his naming of the post commandants who were allowed to trade brandy by these authorities—was deleted in its entirety.

While Surlaville included the essence of Raymond's evidence on rampant favoritism, he omitted the names of those individuals and families identified by Raymond (NAC 2929) as being favored by the authorities. Similarly, he deleted the name of Abbé François Picquet, the Sulpician priest who founded La Présentation and the subject of a diatribe by Raymond (NAC 2897; 2965-67), while adopting (NAC 3014-15) Raymond's position that the king grant the post as a concession rather than continue to pay its expenses. Surlaville reduced Raymond's more than three bitter pages to the following three paragraphs:

This fort is 40 leagues from *Montreal*, on the *Frontenac* River, at the place named La *Galette*. It is utterly useless. Its construction and all its outbuildings have cost and each day cost the king immense sums which are a complete loss. One would like to be able to imagine the motives that led the court to order the establishment of this fort.

One imagines that religious goals created the idea of building it. It has been said that the outcome is very misleading, then, as this post has served until now only to provide a refuge for some old Indians, some licentious Indian women, some disreputable and useless people who are kept there at the king's expense.

It would be desirable for this fort to be awarded as soon as possible as a grant to the people who conceived at court the plan to build it. This would spare His Majesty many expenses.

Surlaville's rendering of Raymond's discourse on the Abbé Picquet's settlement is representative of the manner in which he gathered together, reduced, depersonalized, and recast most of Raymond's discursive material. In justice to Raymond, he was writing to someone he considered a trusted friend and patron, to whom he wrote on the first page of his *dénombrement*, "Do not expect a polished report with each word weighed as if it were to be placed under the eyes of a minister."

In reducing and recasting Raymond's report to a less dramatic and less colorful document, Surlaville did on occasion make use of his own imagery. Compare, for example, Surlaville's version (NAC 3025-26, translated below) of a portion of Raymond's long and rather eloquent plea (NAC 2929-30) to raise the income of the drastically underpaid captains by rotating the posts' commands among them:

It would consequently be very necessary for the court to look carefully at the lowness of the pay that it gives to the French and Canadian officers serving in that colony.

The captains are only paid 1,062 livres. How can they support themselves and their families with that? The lowest captain who is not married is obliged to pay 1,200 livres for room and board without a servant, and 1,600 livres with a servant. Where can they obtain the difference in a country where the price of everything is prohibitive?

The officer finds himself reduced to the dire necessity of resorting to borrowing. Merchants sometimes consent to their needs after many appeals because of their legitimate fear of often losing their debtors and their claims. The court could obviate this difficulty by increasing the officers' regular pay and supplementary pay, which it could do with no additional expense by the means that will be spelled out in the remainder of these remarks.

We have just provided one [means] in proposing that the officers, captains, be assigned in turn to the various commands. Those who have no resources to support themselves decently and with dignity would find assistance in these assignments by means of the supplementary pay which would be attached to them. Henceforth they would no longer see themselves exposed to the scorn of the soldiers and of the people, whose piercing eyes make the indigence and destitution of those who command them stand out only too clearly. Then their authority is weakened, they are obliged to loosen up, discipline weakens; it is difficult to remain resolute for long against people one needs.

The excerpt just cited illustrates again both the relatively low-key rhetoric employed by Surlaville and the great similarity of his content to Raymond's. Here, however, he could not resist adding his own personal touch to his version by envisioning himself in the shoes of an impoverished and scorned captain standing before the "piercing eyes" of his subordinates and even the common people.

Raymond expected Surlaville to weigh the latter's own words when he communicated the information to the minister, and the colonel did not disappoint him. At the same time, by his judicious deletions, Surlaville minimized the possibility of antagonizing in New France (and France) members of the elite families, the bishop of Quebec, the clergy, the governor general, the intendant, and various officers and their friends and allies. His discretion and political sense are evident here, qualities that certainly helped him rise to the rank of general.[3]

Surlaville clearly spent much time in carefully transposing the *dénombrement* to his own *mémoire*. In addition to rewriting and reorganizing, he did from time to time add his own thinking on various matters. For example, his change of Raymond's wording regarding the English presence in the Ohio River is interesting: Raymond spoke (NAC 2917) of having French-allied Indians "chase the English out of Chöaguin and the Belle Rivière [Oswego and the Ohio River]," implying that the English were encroaching on territory that was (or should be) French, whereas Surlaville wrote (NAC 3007) that "Once Oswego and the Ohio River are taken from the English, all the Indian nations will run in crowds to the French posts."[4] Did Surlaville believe that the English had more of a claim on these locations than the French? Even Louis Coulon de Villiers, who defeated Washington at Fort Necessity in 1754, was not certain that the English had no rights in the Ohio River Valley. This was surely the reason that Villiers blundered in writing the sixth article of capitulation, in which he gave the English permission to return to the Ohio after one year.[5]

Despite his great care, Surlaville appears to have misunderstood Raymond's convoluted and syntactically incorrect description of the illicit fur trading at the king's post of Niagara (NAC 2919-20). In attempting to recast clearly Raymond's garbled sentence, Surlaville wrote, "They [the king's appointees at Niagara] send to Oswego and to the other English posts by voyageurs and by even trusted Indians the furs and beaver *which come to them from Montreal via Detroit . . .*" [emphasis added]. This surely is not logical in terms of the geographical locations in question. I have concluded from Raymond's passage that the Niagara personnel sent beaver pelts to Oswego that they themselves had traded at Niagara, rather than, as ordered, sending them all down to Montreal with the voyageurs going from Detroit to Montreal via Niagara. (See note 51 of the *dénombrement* translation in part III, on pp. 127-28, for the transcription of both Raymond's and Surlaville's French and a more detailed analysis of this passage.)

In 1754, Raymond knew that exposing the irregularities he had observed in New France placed him in jeopardy. Regarding Picquet and La Présentation, he wrote (NAC 2967) "In giving you a detailed account of Canada I am running the risk of being excommunicated and making irreconcilable enemies for myself." In closing his report (NAC 2982), he entreated Surlaville, "If you expose me to Canadian vengeance, become my protector." His identity was not revealed by Surlaville, who clearly supported him at court, but Raymond never saw his plan implemented nor did he receive a lucrative assignment from Governor General Duquesne.

While Raymond's fierce criticisms against officials and clergy were deleted or toned down in the version submitted to the minister, his analysis and proposed solution were adopted and forwarded by his highly placed friend. As Aegidius Fauteux observed in 1928, Surlaville's *mémoire* "is not an absolutely exact reproduction of the preceding [piece by Raymond], but it is substantially faithful to it."[6] The erupting French and Indian War, with New France besieged on all sides, became the overriding priority for the French command, and (Raymond's and) Surlaville's recommendations became less imperative. A French post was built at the Petit Rapide in 1758, but it remained in French hands for only one year, being destroyed after Niagara fell to the British in 1759.[7] The increasingly desperate struggle and subsequent unraveling of the French North American empire precluded further consideration of the sweeping revisions proposed initially by Raymond, but his *dénombrement* remains today a rich source of new information on conditions in the posts of New France on the eve of its conquest.

NOTES

1. T. A. Crowley, "Le Courtois de Surlaville (Le Courtois de Blais de Surlaville), Michel," *Dictionary of Canadian Biography* (hereafter cited as *DCB*) 12 vols. (Toronto: University of Toronto Press, 1966-91), 4:443.

2. Gaston Du Boscq de Beaumont, *Les derniers jours de l'Acadie (1748-1758): Correspondances et mémoires* (Paris, 1899; reprint Geneva: Slatkine-Megariotis Reprints, 1975), 279, 280.

3. According to Du Boscq de Beaumont (*Les derniers Jours de l'Acadie*, 3), Surlaville was named major general in 1754; T. A. Crowley, "Courtois de Surlaville" (*DCB*, 4:444), stated, however, that he was promoted to brigadier in 1761.

4. Surlaville wrote: *Chouaguin et Belle rivière une fois Enlevés aux anglois les Nations sauvages accouréront [sic] en foule aux postes françois.*

5. See Joseph L. Peyser, *Letters from New France: The Upper Country 1686-1783* (Urbana: University of Illinois Press), 205-7 for an English-language translation of the surrender terms.

6. Aegidius Fautex, "Le chevalier de Raymond," *Rapport de l'archiviste de la province de Québec, 1927-1928*, 317.

7. Daniel Chabert-Joncaire, *Mémoire pour Daniel de la Joncaire-Chabert, ci-devant commandant au petit Fort de Niagara contre M. le procureur-général de la commission établie pour l'affaire du Canada* (S.l.: Imprimerie de Grange, ca. 1763, 3 parts in 1 volume), part 3:4n; "Buffalo," *Encyclopedia Americana*, 30 vols. (New York: Americana Corporation, 1954), 4:691.

APPENDIX 1
TOPICAL OUTLINE OF
SURLAVILLE'S *MÉMOIRE*

The structure of Surlaville's *mémoire* is straightforward. His major divisions, many of which correspond exactly to Raymond's, are clearly headed by centered bold lettering, rendered in boldface type in the following outline. The numbers in square brackets identify the National Archives of Canada transcript page numbers on which the indicated material is located. Roman and, with few exceptions (marked by asterisks), Arabic numerals are mine.

STRUCTURE OF SURLAVILLE'S *MÉMOIRE*

Introduction to his **Mémoire en forme d'observations** listing three groups of observations on the Canadian posts [NAC 2998]:

*1. The list of posts with their locations; the communication links they have with one another;
*2. The selection of their commandants; the character of the Indians; the way to deal with them; description of the garrisons and of the posts that should have them; the means of increasing the officers' pay and of maintaining the troops without any new expense for the king; the possibility provided by this means to greatly increase the king's income;
*3. The present cost of provisioning the troops maintained in this colony in the king's service.

    I. List of the Posts [NAC 2998-3015]
       A. **Northern Posts** [NAC 2998-99]
       B. **Southern Posts** [NAC 2999-3000]
       C. **Detroit** [NAC 3001-2]
       D. **Michilimackinac** [NAC 3002-6]
          Plan for fortifying and holding three key passages to control the fur trade and retain the upper country

E. **The Petit Rapide** [NAC 3006-14]
    Importance of the Petit Rapide [NAC 3008-12], including a con-
    fused *"petite digression"* on the illicit fur trade between Niagara and
    Oswego [NAC 3008-9]; Raymond's proposed water-transportation
    system [NAC 3009-11]; considerations on the threat of English
    invasions from Oswego and Acadia in order to "totally chase the
    French out of Canada" [NAC 3012-14]
F. **La Présentation** [NAC 3014-15]

II. Related Topics [NAC 3015-48]
    A. **Selection of Commandants for the Canadian
        posts** [NAC 3015-17]
    B. **Character of the Indians** [NAC 3017-26]
        Their nature [NAC 3017-22]; ways to deal with the Indians and
        to avoid dishonesty and trading by the officers [NAC 3022-26]
    C   **Expedient** [NAC 3026-43]
        The means for increasing officers' pay and maintaining troops with-
        out any new expense to the king [NAC 3026-32]; present cost at
        Detroit of food for the troops in the upper country [NAC 3032-
        33]; considerations regarding the posts' officers and employees and
        statement of costs to maintain them [NAC 3034-43]
    D. **Garrisons and Locations Where It Would Be
        Appropriate to Have Them** [NAC 3043-45]
    E. **Regulation of the Congés Established in Each Post**
        [NAC 3035-48]
            1. **Northern Posts** [NAC 3046]
            2. **Southern Posts** [NAC 3047]
            3. Acadian Trade and Fishing [NAC 3047-48]

III. **Present Costs of Maintaining**
      1. **The Troops** (and Employees) [NAC 3048-53]
      *2. **The Barks** [NAC 3053-54]

IV. **Statement of Account** [NAC 3054-55]
    Income and expenses of the proposed system and possible
    profit for the king

*These Arabic numerals were used by Surlaville.

APPENDIX 2
ANNOTATED TRANSLATION
OF AEGIDIUS FAUTEUX'S LE
CHEVALIER DE RAYMOND

The following report comes from the archives of the Séminaire de Saint-Sulpice in Paris, where we discovered it during the course of research done during the summer of 1923. It is part of a diverse collection of handwritten documents entitled *Pièces pour l'histoire militaire du Canada, 1730-1760*, and covers no less than 72 large folio pages.

There are neither title, nor signature, nor date, but the writing and the paper indicate sufficiently that we are in the presence of an old document going back to the end of the French régime. These are the observations of an officer of the Marine [colonial troops] on the organization of the posts of Canada at the time of Governor Duquesne.[1]

Directly alongside of it, in the same volume, is found the same report, but reduced to 68 pages in-folio. This second piece, of official nature, is titled "Report in the form of observations concerning 1) the enumeration of the posts of Canada; 2) the selection of the commandants; 3) the maintenance of the troops."[2] It is not an absolutely exact reproduction of the preceding one, but it is substantially faithful to it. Contrary to the first one it is carefully written in a beautiful professional handwriting.[3] It is obviously a copy of the original document done by a writer in the Marine to be submitted to the minister of the colonies. The phraseology is often quite different, the spelling is a little less fanciful, and everything that pertains personally to the author in the first writing has been deleted.

Precisely because it is more complete than the one submitted to the minister and because it is at the same time livelier, we have preferred to reproduce the report here just as it came from its author's pen.[4]

By whom had this anonymous report been drawn up, and in what period? These were the first two problems to resolve.

151

The date itself is quite easy to establish. In one place, the author speaks of "two million [livres] used up for two thousand men who were made to march last year to build Fort Presqu'ile and the one at the Rivière aux Boeufs out of wood, and this year the one named Fort Duquesne, for the building of which and M. de Villiers' detachment which was going to avenge the death of his brother, around 1,500 men were made to march." It is therefore in 1754, the year of the surrender of Fort Necessity, that our report was written.

Although it was a little less easy to determine the author, we nonetheless succeeded without too much difficulty, thanks to two or three personal allusions that the text provided to us. By his own admission, the officer who was holding the pen had been serving His Majesty for 32 years in the troops of Canada, had commanded the Niagara post and the one at the Miamis at different periods, and was replaced at the Niagara post by M. de Beaujeu under M. de la Galissonnière [*sic*].[5] One does not need more to recognize the Chevalier de Raymond, who, in fact, in the year 1754, had been serving for 32 years, having come to Canada and having been made an ensign in 1722; and who, after having been commandant at Niagara for the first time in 1748, was replaced there in 1749 by M. de Beaujeu as he [Raymond] was going to take command of the Miami post.

If more ample proof were needed in addition, we would find it in Surlaville's papers which were partially published by the author of *Les derniers jours de l'Acadie* (The Last Days of Acadia). Indeed, M. DuBoscq [*sic*] de Beaumont reproduced as an appendix to his work, and under the title *Observations à faire sur le choix des commandants des postes* (Observations to Be Made on the Selection of the Post Commandants), some pages from a document that was signed *de Raymond*, and these pages correspond exactly, if not to the text that we are publishing here, at least to the official writing about which we have spoken above and which had been done for the minister's information.[6] The report of which M. de Beaumont published only a short fragment should be found complete in Surlaville's papers, for, as is evident from the first line of the text that we are publishing here, it is to the former major of troops of Ile Royale, Le Courtois de Surlaville, that it was originally sent.

A few biographical notes on the Chevalier de Raymond will help, we believe, to make both the motives that inspired him to write his report and the reasons that made him select M. de Surlaville as his addressee more understandable.

Charles de Raymond belonged to an old family whose branches were established in [the regions of] Périgord, Quercy, Angoumois, Agenais, and Saintonge.[7] He was born in Saintonge around 1706. We believe he was the son of Louis de Raymond and Marguerite-Louise Amelotte. At the time of his marriage in 1697, his father was seigneur of Rivières and of Grandpré, in the parish of Saint-Aignan, and a lieutenant in the Champagne Regiment; but in another record, in 1714, he is described as seigneur of Le Carlos in the parish of Moutierneuf.

Whatever the case, Charles came to Canada for the first time in 1722, with a commission as second ensign having been granted him upon the recommendation of the Count of Evreux. From that date until the cession of the country in 1760, that is to say for 38 years, he appears to have left only three times to go to France: the first time from 1725 to 1728, the second in 1746 and the third in 1753. Promoted to full ensign in 1731, he was made a lieutenant in the *Troupes de la Marine* on 6 May 1738, and the Marquis de Beauharnois immediately entrusted the command of the Niagara post to him, which he kept until 1746.[8]

In this same year, 1746, he was finally provided with a company.[9] After having taken part in 1746 in M. de Rigaud's expedition against New England,[10] he was again called to the Niagara command by M. de la Galissonnière in 1748. The following year he was replaced at Niagara by M. de Beaujeu and assumed command of the Miami post, only to be relieved of it in 1751[11] by M. de La Jonquière. In 1752, his company was one of two that the governor of Canada loaned to the government of Ile Royale [Cape Breton Island]. The Count de Raymond,[12] who had just been named governor of Ile Royale, was not the brother, as we read in the *Rapport des Archives Canadiennes pour 1905*, no doubt according to a faulty transcript (I, 292), but a cousin of the captain of the Canadian troops. It was obviously this kinship that impelled M. de La Jonquière to select the Chevalier de Raymond as one of the two officers designated for Ile Royale. The latter spent only a short time at Louisbourg; without considering the fact that he followed his company there only at the end of 1752, he was already going back to France in October 1753 with the Count de Raymond and M. de Surlaville. Back at Louisbourg on 2 August 1754, he was already back in Quebec in the following October to no longer serve anywhere but in Canada. We find him in 1755 at the Battle of Lake George with M. Dieskau and, in 1758, at the Battle of Ticonderoga, where he commanded the colonial troops and performed with such distinction that he earned both the praise of Montcalm and a pension of 300 livres from the royal treasury.[13]

He was supposed to be made a knight [*chevalier*] of Saint Louis in 1753, but as he was in France when the king's letters reached M. Duquesne, he could be admitted only in 1754 according to new letters sent to M. de La Galissonière in France itself. The Chevalier de Raymond went back to France after the capitulation, withdrew from the service, and settled in Saintes. He died there in February 1774 at the surgeon Vivier's and was buried at Sainte-Colombe. Nothing indicates that he ever married; however M. Dangibeaud, in his *Minutes de notaire de la Saintonge* (II, 237), mentions a record of 1743 in which Elizabeth de Raymond, daughter of Charles de Raymond, an officer in the troops of the Marine detachment at Quebec, is mentioned.

The Chevalier de Raymond, when he sent his observations to M. de Surlaville with the obvious intention of reaching the minister himself by means of this intervention, was not as disinterested as he wanted to appear. His report is a veritable plea for his own case;[14] he is filled with bitterness regarding his comrades who are stuffing themselves while he fasts and it is basically but a continual sigh for an appointment in which he will be able to get rich. Since the beginning, moreover, he appears to have been a great beggar. In 1736 and in 1742, the minister had to reply to him that it was useless for him to appeal in France and that it was to M. de Beauharnois that he had to speak if he wished to be a post commander. In October 1751, after his recall from the Miami post, he again sent a report to the minister in which one can already find the broad features of the project that the presently published report displays and in which he requested the command of the La Baie post [Green Bay, Wisconsin] for a period of six years with no remuneration other than the freedom to exploit it.[15] Unfortunately, he did not succeed in overcoming the obduracy of M. Duquesne, who was not willing to believe in the indispensability of his services. To a more particularly insistent ministerial recommendation, the governor did not hesitate to reply, on 7 October 1753 [*sic*],[16] that Sieur de Raymond had already earned a lot of money at the Miami post and that his pretensions were greatly exaggerated. In April 1754 the minister wrote once again to Duquesne in order to recommend the chevalier, who was then in France, to him. "I shall be very pleased," he wrote, "if you can give him a special command, if you have the opportunity, seeing that he is strongly recommended by highly regarded important individuals."[17]

It was no doubt this latest recommendation that the Chevalier de Raymond, in his letter of 28 October 1754, declared had been so poorly received by the governor. "M. Duquesne," he wrote, "looked upon the letter of recommendation that the minister had given me as if it were a song from the Pont-Neuf."[18] Perhaps also this was the very rebuff which caused the chevalier to put forth a supreme effort by summing up all his arguments in the report presented here, for everything indicates that the report was written at the end of 1754, after the return of its author to Quebec. The allusion to the taking of Fort Necessity cannot be explained otherwise. That event took place in July 1754 in fact, and Sieur de Raymond who was at that time on the high seas could have known about it only upon his return.

Now why did M. de Raymond confide in M. de Surlaville rather than another? It was because at that time the ex-major of the troops of Ile Royale was extremely well connected at court. He was the protégé, and one could almost say the friend of the famous Duke de Choiseul who, during almost the whole reign of Mme de Pompadour, was an all-powerful minister at Louis XV's court.[19] The Chevalier de Raymond, who had known Surlaville at Louisbourg and who made the trip from Ile Royale to France on the same ship in 1753, certainly did not fail to court him and seek his support. And he did not believe he could find a better intermediary than "my dear Surlaville" to get right to the minister.

These remarks appeared necessary to us to help sort out what might be exaggerated on the one hand and well founded on the other in a report like the one reproduced here. This distinction made, it seemed to us that the observations of the Chevalier de Raymond still remained an invaluable document to consult for the history of the posts at the end of the French régime and that, for the benefit of our historians, it deserved to be published in its entirety.

Aegidius Fauteux

NOTES

This article was written as an introduction to Fauteux's French-language transcript of Raymond's *dénombrement de tous les postes du Canada*, published in the *Rapport de l'archiviste de la province de Québec pour 1927-28* (Quebec: L.-A. Proulx, Imprimeur de Sa Majesté le Roi). The introduction to the article, titled simply "Le Chevalier de Raymond," is on pages 317-22, and the transcript, titled by Fauteux *Mémoire sur les postes du Canada adressé à M. de Surlaville, en 1754, par le Chevalier de Raymond*, follows on pages 323-54.

1. The Marquis Ange de Menneville Duquesne was governor general of New France from 1752 to 1755, succeeding Jacques-Pierre Taffanel de La Jonquière.

2. *Mémoire en forme d'observations concernant 1) le dénombrement des postes du Canada; 2) le choix des commandants; 3) le traitement des troupes.* Actually, Fauteux shortened Surlaville's very lengthy title, which fully translated reads: "Report in the form of observations concerning 1) the posts of Canada, their locations, the linkage that one and another have with each other, the advantages that can reasonably be expected from them; 2) The selection of the commandants of these posts, the character of the Indians in these parts, the manner of dealing with them, the state of the garrisons and the posts where it is appropriate to have them, the means of increasing the supplementary pay granted the officers and of maintaining the troops without any new expense for the king, the possibilities that this means would create to increase considerably His Majesty's income; 3) The present upkeep of the troops maintained in this colony in the king's service."

3. Contrary to Fauteux's statement, the Séminaire de Saint-Sulpice's copy of Raymond's report is also written in a beautiful hand. Neither appear to be originals. The register in question does, however, also contain a relatively poorly penned copy of Surlaville's report, apparently identical in content to the copy mentioned by Fauteux. This version, labeled Pièce 40, nearer the back of the volume, is not in Surlaville's handwriting. The copy discussed by Fauteux is labeled Pièce 38. The location of Raymond's original report is not known.

4. This is misleading: Fauteux divided Raymond's interminable paragraphs into shorter ones; he corrected many of the errors in spelling; he modernized the imperfect verb endings; he corrected grammatical errors; and he occasionally changed Raymond's wording. Some of his corrections and changes are illustrated here: *ses* became *ces*; *quant resulte il?* became *qu'en résulte-t-il?*; *arrête* became *arrêtent*; *setendent* became *s'étend*; *on en fait pas pour vous* became *on n'en fait pas pour vous*; *marchands* became *marchandises*. Fauteux's transcript also omitted the phrase *de bled deinde ou bled de turquis et des graisses d'ours* (NAC 2910).

5. Daniel-Hyacinthe-Marie Liénard de Beaujeu had a distinguished military career during King George's War (1744-48) and in the French and Indian War, during which he died in 1755 heroically leading his outnumbered detachment against Braddock. The Marquis Roland-Michel Barrin de La Galissonière served as commandant general of New France from 1747 to 1749 in place of Governor General Jacques-Pierre de Taffanel de La Jonquière, who had been captured in a naval battle with the English.

6. Fauteux overstated the case when he wrote that the pages written by Raymond and published by Gaston Du Boscq de Beaumont in his *Les derniers jours de l'Acadie (1748-1758): Correspondances et mémoires* (Paris: 1899; reprint Geneva: Slatkine-Megariotis Reprints, 1975), 275-81, *correspondent exactement . . . à la rédaction officielle* written by Surlaville. There is no question about the material and views in these documents being very similar, or that their source is Charles de

Raymond, but my examination of all the documents in question did not find the exactitude reported by Fauteux.

7. These regions are in the southwestern part of France.

8. The *Troupes de la Marine* were the regular colonial troops in Canada. The Marquis Charles de La Boische de Beauharnois was governor general of New France from 1726 to 1747.

9. That is, he was promoted to the rank of captain.

10. François-Pierre Rigaud de Vaudreuil, son of one governor general of New France (Philippe de Rigaud de Vaudreuil, 1703-25) and brother of another (Pierre de Rigaud de Vaudreuil de Cavagnial, 1755-60), led a successful raid into New York and Massachusetts in the summer of 1746 (Jean Hamelin and Jacqueline Roy, "Rigaud de Vaudreuil, François-Pierre de," *Dictionary of Canadian Biography* [hereafter cited as *DCB*], 12 vols. [Toronto: University of Toronto Press, 1966-91], 4:66).

11. The year is in error. Raymond was recalled from the Miami post in 1750. See part I, notes 1, 33, and 38, for details and documentation.

12. The Count Jean-Louis de Raymond governed Ile Royale from 1751 to 1753. Throughout his career his energies were devoted to "personal advancement rather than public service" according to T. A. Crowley's rather unflattering biography of him in the *DCB*, 4:655-57. One wonders in reading Charles de Raymond's *dénombrement* if having this goal was a family trait shared by the two cousins.

13. The Battle of Lake George is known in French as *la bataille du lac Saint-Sacrement*; the Battle of Ticonderoga is *la bataille de Carillon*. Baron Jean-Armand Dieskau was named in 1755 as commander of the French regular troops sent to Canada. Dieskau was badly wounded and captured by the British at the Battle of Lake George, which ended as a stalemate. In 1756 the Marquis Louis-Joseph de Montcalm arrived in America as Dieskau's replacement as commander of the French regulars. He was credited with the great victory of the French over the British at Ticonderoga in 1758.

14. Fauteux wrote here *un véritable plaidoyer pro domo*.

15. Fauteux's footnote here reads, "Canada, Corresp. générale, C II, vol. 95, fol. 389." The volume cited is in error, Raymond's 1 October 1751 letter being in AN Col., C^{11}A, 97:389. The French transcript of this letter is in the National Archives of Canada (hereafter cited as NAC), Manuscript Division microfilm C 2399, pp. 296-305; the English translation is in the *Collections of the State Historical Society of Wisconsin*, 20 vols. (Madison: State Historical Society of Wisconsin, 1855-1911), 18:94-98. In this letter to Count Antoine-Louis Rouillé, secretary and minister of state, Raymond first provides an account of his service from 1722 to his assignment to the Miami post. He then provides the details of his command of that troubled post, his "unjust" recall, and his replacement by Louis Coulon de Villiers who, Raymond accurately states, did no better than he. He

concludes by requesting command of Michilimackinac with the rank of major, with the congés for that post going to him as his remuneration, or command of the Green Bay post for six years.

16. The year is in error; Duquesne's letter to the minister was dated 7 October 1754. It is in AN Col. C^{11}A, 99:257 (NAC microfilm C 2400, transcript pp. 258-59.) The complete letter is translated in part I of this volume.

17. Fauteux's misreading of the date of Duquesne's letter caused him to reverse their order. Duquesne's 7 October 1754 letter was in response to the minister's strong recommendation written to him on 18 April 1754. Regarding the content of the minister's letter to Duquesne, despite the use of quotation marks, Fauteux substantially changed the wording, even though he retained the minister's meaning as expressed elsewhere in the letter. The minister's words in his last sentence were *Et je serai bien aise d'ailleurs que vous puissiez faire quelque chose pour luy, par raport [sic] à plusieurs personnes de considération à qui il appartient et qui me l'ont fort recommandé.* Fauteux's transcription of these words was *Je serai bien aise que vous puissiez lui donner un commandement particulier, si vous en avez l'occasion, attendu qu'il est fortement recommandé par des personnages de haute considération.* The minister's complete letter (Minister to Duquesne, Versailles, 18 April 1754, AN Col. B, 99:180 [NAC microfilm C 15660, transcript p. 41]) is translated in part I of this volume.

18. Fauteux's footnote here is "DuBoscq de Beaumont, *Derniers jours de l'Acadie,* p. 130." The quotation from this letter, which is excerpted in the book, is accurate. The Pont-Neuf, "New Bridge," which crosses the Seine in the heart of Paris, was constructed from 1578 to 1606. For many years it was the locus of traveling theater troupes, acrobats, and clowns. Raymond's simile is a colorful if bitter way to describe the governor's scorn vis-à-vis the minister's recommendation. See "Pont-Neuf," 4:2459, and "Tréteaux," 5:3066, *Grand Larousse en 5 volumes* (Paris: Librairie Larousse, 1987).

19. Etienne-François Choiseul became a major general in 1748, ambassador to Rome in 1754, and ambassador to Vienna in 1757. He was elevated to duke in 1758 when he became minister of foreign affairs. He was named minister of war and minister of the Marine in 1761, and was *de facto* prime minister until 1770, when he fell from grace several years after the death of Mme de Pompadour (*Grand Larousse en 5 volumes,* 1:639).

BIBLIOGRAPHY

Manuscript Sources

Aix-en-Provence. Archives nationales (France).
    Centre des Archives d'Outre-Mer. Dépôt des fortifications des
    Colonies (Amérique septentrionale).

Ann Arbor. University of Michigan. William L. Clements Library.
    Book Division.
    Map Division.

Cambridge, Massachusetts. Harvard University. Houghton Library.
    Manuscript Department.

Montreal. Archives nationales du Québec à Montréal.
    Greffe de Danré de Blanzy

New York. New York Public Library.
    Book Division.

Oka, Quebec. Paroisse de l'Annonciation.

Ottawa. National Archives of Canada.
    Archives françaises, Division des manuscrits.
        Fonds MG 1, Archives des Colonies (Paris).
            Série B, Lettres envoyées. vol. 99 (transcriptions)
            Série $C^{11}A$, Correspondance générale, Canada, vols. 93, 95,
                96, 97, 99 (transcriptions).
        Fonds MG 5, Ministère des Affaires étrangères (Paris).
            B. Mémoires et documents.
                1.   Amérique, vol. 11 (transcriptions).

159

Fonds MG 17, Archives religieuses.
    A: Eglise catholique, 7-1, vol. 4 (transcriptions).
Cartographic and Architectural Division.
Visual and Sound Archives, Art Acquisition and Research..

Paris. Archives nationales.
    Les fonds des Colonies antérieurs à 1815.
        Série B, Correspondance au départ.
            vols. 22, 99.
        Sous-série $C^{11}A$, Correspondance à l'arrivée.
            vols. 67, 87, 97, 116, 119, 124.
        Sous-série $C^{11}E$, Des limites et des postes
            vol. 13.

Paris. Archives du Séminaire de Saint-Sulpice.
    Manuscrit 1200, pièces 35, 38, 40.

Quebec. Archives nationales du Québec.
    Greffe de Jean-Baptiste Adhémar dit St.-Martin.

Quebec. Musée de la civilisation.
    Fonds d'archives du Séminaire de Québec.
        Article CR-1941-271
        Fonds Verreau, carton 5
        Papiers de Surlaville, *Polygraphie* n° 55, 56, 57, 58.

Vincennes, France. Service historique de la Marine.
    Recueil N° 67.

PRINTED SOURCES

Adams, Blaine. "Le Provost Duquesnel (Du Quesnel), Jean- Baptiste."
    Dictionary of Canadian Biography. 12 vols. Toronto: University of
    Toronto Press, 1966-91, 3:392.
Allaire, Gratien. "Officiers et marchands: Les sociétés de commerce des
    fourrures, 1715-1760." *Revue d'histoire de l'Amérique française* 40, no. 3
    (1987): 409-27.

Armour, David A., ed. *Attack at Michilimackinac: Alexander Henry's Travels and Adventures in Canada and the Indian Territories between the Years 1760 and 1764.* Mackinac Island: Mackinac Island State Park Commission, 1971.

Beaudet, Pierre, and Céline Cloutier. *Archaeology at Fort Chambly,* Studies in Archaeology, Architecture and History. Ottawa: Canadian Parks Service, 1989.

Bosher, John F., and Jean-Claude Dubé. "Bigot, François." *Dictionary of Canadian Biography,* 4:59-71.

Bougainville, Louis-Antoine de. Letter to Madame Herault de Seychelles. 8 November 1757. *Bulletin des recherches historiques,* 37:456.

Brigham, William B. "The Grand Kickapoo Village and Associated Fort in the Illinois Wilderness." *Indian Mounds and Villages.* Bulletin No. 2, Illinois Archaeological Survey. Urbana: University of Illinois, 1960.

Burpee, Lawrence J. Jr. *Journals and Letters of Pierre Gaultier de Varennes de La Vérendrye and His Sons.* Toronto: Champlain Society, 1927.

Casgrain, Henri-Raymond. *Guerre du Canada, 1756-1760, Montcalm et Lévis.* vol. 1. Quebec: Demers et Frères, 1891.

Champagne, Antoine. *Nouvelles études sur les La Vérendrye et le poste de l'ouest.* Quebec: Les Presses de l'Université Laval, 1971.

Chartrand, René. *Canadian Military Heritage.* vol. 1. Montreal: Art Global, Inc., 1993.

Clark, Andrew Hill. *Acadia: The Geography of Early Nova Scotia to 1760.* Madison: University of Wisconsin Press, 1968.

Collections of the State Historical Society of Wisconsin. 20 vols. Madison: State Historical Society of Wisconsin, 1854-1911.

Colley, Linda. *Britons: Forging the Nation 1707-1837.* New Haven, Conn.: Yale University Press, 1992.

Cooper, Johnson Gaylord. "Oswego in the French-English Struggle in North America." Ph.D. diss., Syracuse University, 1961.

Cossette, Joseph. "Bonnécamps, Joseph-Pierre de." *Dictionary of Canadian Biography,* 4:76-77.

Côté, Pierre-L. "Duquesne (Du Quesne, Duquaine, Duquêne) de Menneville, Ange, Marquis Duquesne." *Dictionary of Canadian Biography,* 4:255-58.

Cotgrave, Randle. *A Dictionarie of the French and English Tongues.* London: Adam Islip, 1611; reprint, Columbia: University of South Carolina Press, 1968.

Crisman, Kevin J. "Struggle for a Continent: Naval Battles of the French and Indian Wars." Pp. 132-33 in *Ships and Shipwrecks of the Americas: A*

History Based on Underwater Archaeology, ed. George E. Buss. New York: Thames and Hudson, 1988.

Crowley, T.A. "Le Courtois de Surlaville (Le Courtois de Blais de Surlaville), Michel." *Dictionary of Canadian Biography*, 4:443-44.

Dickinson, John A. "La Justice seigneuriale en Nouvelle-France: le cas de Notre-Dame-des-Anges." *Revue d'histoire de l'Amérique française*. 28, no. 3 (décembre 1974): 323-46.

Dictionary of Canadian Biography (DCB). 12 vols. Toronto: University of Toronto Press, 1966-91.

Dinel, Guy. "Péan, Michel-Jean-Hugues." *Dictionary of Canadian Biography*, 4:614-17.

Du Boscq de Beaumont, Gaston. *Les derniers jours de l'Acadie (1748-1758): Correspondances et Mémoires*. Paris, 1899; reprint, Geneva: Slatkine-Megariotis Reprints, 1975.

Dunn, Walter S. Jr. "Chabert de Joncaire de Clausonne, Daniel-Marie." *Dictionary of Canadian Biography*, 4:137-38.

Dunnigan, Brian Leigh. *Glorious Old Relic: The French Castle and Old Fort Niagara*. Youngstown, N.Y.: Old Fort Niagara Assoc., 1987.

Eccles, W. J. *The Canadian Frontier 1534-1760*, rev. ed. Albuquerque: University of New Mexico Press, 1983.

_____. "Céloron de Blainville, Pierre-Joseph." *Dictionary of Canadian Biography*, 3:99-100.

_____.*France in America*, rev. ed. East Lansing: Michigan State University Press, 1990.

_____. "The French Forces in North America during the Seven Years' War." *Dictionary of Canadian Biography*, 3:xvii.

_____. "Marin de La Malgue (La Marque), Paul." *Dictionary of Canadian Biography*, 3:431-32.

_____. "Sovereignty Association, 1500-1783." *Canadian Historical Review* 65, no. 4 (December 1984): 475-510.

Edmunds, R. David. "A History of the Kickapoo Indians in Illinois from 1750-1834." Master's thesis, Illinois State University, 1966.

Edmunds, R. David, and Joseph L. Peyser. *The Fox Wars: The Mesquakie Challenge to New France*. Norman: University of Oklahoma Press, 1993.

E[inhorn], A[rthur]. "Six Nations Confederacy." *Dictionary of Canadian Biography,* 3:xli.

Encyclopedia Americana, 1954 ed., s.v. "Buffalo."

Fairchild, Byron. "Pepperrell, Sir William," *Dictionary of Canadian Biography,* 3:505-9.

Fauteux, Aegidius. "Le chevalier de Raymond." *Rapport de l'archiviste de la province de Québec pour 1927-1928.* Quebec: L.-A. Proulx, Imprimeur de Sa Majesté le Roi, 319-20.

_____. *Les Chevaliers de Saint-Louis en Canada.* Montreal: Les Editions des Dix, 1940.

_____. "Mémoire sur les postes du Canada adressé à M. de Surlaville, en 1754, par le Chevalier de Raymond." *Rapport l'archiviste de la province de Québec pour 1927-1928.* Québec: L.-A. Proulx, Imprimeur de Sa Majesté le Roi, 323-54.

Finn, Gérard. "Le Loutre, Jean-Louis." *Dictionary of Canadian Biography,* 4:453-58.

Gélinsas, Cyrille. *The Role of Fort Chambly in the Development of New France.* Studies in Archaeology, Architecture and History. Ottawa: Canadian Parks Service, 1983.

Genêt, Nicole, Luce Vermette, and Louise Décarie-Audet. *Les objets familiers de nos ancêtres.* Montreal: Les Editions de l'homme, 1974.

Gérin-Lajoie, Marie, trans. and ed. "Fort Michilimackinac in 1749: Lotbinière's Plan and Description." *Mackinac History Series,* vol. 2, leaflet no. 5. Mackinac Island: Mackinac Island State Park Commission, 1976.

Ghere, David L. "Diplomacy & War on the Maine Frontier, 1678-1759." Pp. 120-42 in *Maine: The Pine Tree State from Prehistory to the Present,* edited by Richard W. Judd, Edwin A. Churchill, and Joel W. Eastman. Orono: University of Maine Press.

Giraud, Marcel. *Histoire de la Louisiane française.* 5 vols. Paris: Presses universitaires de France, 1953-87.

_____. *A History of French Louisiana.* vols. 1, 2, 5. Baton Rouge: Louisiana State University Press, 1974, 1993, 1991.

Grand Larousse en 5 volumes. Paris: Librairie Larousse, 1987.

Halford, Peter W. *Le français des Canadiens à la veille de la Conquête: Témoignage du père Pierre Philippe Potier, s.j.* Ottawa: Les Presses de l'Université d'Ottawa, 1994.

Hamelin, Jean, and Jacqueline Roy. "Rigaud de Vaudreuil, François-Pierre de." *Dictionary of Canadian Biography,* 4:660-62.

Harris, R. Cole, ed. *Historical Atlas of Canada.* vol. 1, "From the Beginning to 1800." Toronto: University of Toronto Press, 1987.

Henry, Alexander. *Travels and Adventures in Canada and the Indian Territories between the Years 1760 and 1776,* 1809; facsimile reprint. Ann Arbor: University Microfilms, 1966.

Hunter, William A. "Orontony (Orontondi, Rondoenie, Wanduny, Nicolas)." *Dictionary of Canadian Biography*, 3:495-96.

_____. "Tanaghrisson (Deanaghrison, Johonerissa, Tanacharison, Tanahisson, Thanayieson and, as a title, the Half King)." *Dictionary of Canadian Biography*, 3:613-15

Idle, Dunning. "The Post of the St. Joseph River during the French Régime 1679-1761." Ph.D. diss., University of Illinois, 1945.

Jaenen, Cornelius J. *The Role of the Church in New France*. Historical Booklet No. 40. Ottawa: Canadian Historical Association, 1985.

_____. *Friend and Foe: Aspects of French-Amerindian Cultural Contact in the Sixteenth and Seventeenth Centuries*. Toronto: McClelland and Stewart, Ltd., 1976.

Jennings, Francis. *Empire of Fortune: Crowns, Colonies, and Tribes in the Seven Years' War in America*. New York: W. W. Norton & Co., 1988.

_____. *Ambiguous Iroquois Empire: The Covenant Chain Confederation of Indian Tribes with English Colonies from its Beginnings to the Lancaster Treaty of 1744*. New York: W. W. Norton & Co., 1984.

Johnson, Micheline D. "Germain, Charles." *Dictionary of Canadian Biography*, 4:289-90.

Joncaire-Chabert, Daniel de. *Mémoire pour Daniel de la Joncaire-Chabert, ci-devant commandant au petit Fort de Niagara contre M. le procureur-général de la commission établie pour l'affaire Du Canada*. 3 parts in 1 vol. No location: Imprimerie de Grange, ca. 1763.

Kalm, Peter. *Travels in North America*, edited by Adolph B. Bensen. 2 vols. New York: Dover Publications, 1964.

Kennett, Lee. *The French Armies in the Seven Years' War*. Durham: Duke University Press, 1967.

Krause, Eric, Carol Corbin, and William O'Shea, eds. *Aspects of Louisbourg*. Sydney, Nova Scotia: University College of Cape Breton Press, 1995.

Lachance, André. *La Justice criminelle du roi au Canada au XVIIIe siècle: Tribunaux et officiers*. Les cahiers d'histoire de l'Université Laval no. 22. Quebec: Les Presses de l'Université Laval, 1978.

_____. "Renaud Dubuisson, Louis-Jacques-Charles." *Dictionary of Canadian Biography*, 3:551-52.

_____. "Varin de La Marre, Jean-Victor." *Dictionary of Canadian Biography*, 4:749-50.

Lahaise, Robert. "Picquet, François." *Dictionary of Canadian Biography*, 4:636-37.

La Société du parler français au Canada. *Glossaire du parler français au Canada*. Quebec: Les Presses de l'Université Laval, 1968.

McConnell, Michael N. *A Country Between: The Upper Ohio Valley and Its Peoples, 1724-1774*. Lincoln: University of Nebraska Press, 1992.

McDermott, John Francis. *A Glossary of Mississippi Valley French 1673-1850*. Washington University Studies—New Series, Language and Literature no. 12. St. Louis: Washington University, 1941.

MacLeod, Malcolm. "Liénard de Beaujeu, Daniel-Hyacinthe-Marie." *Dictionary of Canadian Biography*, 3:400-2.

Miquelon, Dale. *New France 1701-1744: A Supplement to Europe*. Toronto: McClelland & Stewart, Inc., 1987.

Miville-Deschênes, François. *The Soldier Off Duty: Domestic Aspects of Military Life at Fort Chambly under the French Régime as Revealed by Archaeological Objects*. Studies in Archaeology, Architecture and History. Ottawa: Canadian Parks Service, 1987.

Moodie, Edith, trans. English translation (typescript ca. 1890-1914) of Pierre Margry, transcriber and ed., *Découvertes et établissements des Français dans l'ouest et dans le sud de l'Amérique septentrionale 1614-1754: Mémoires et documents inédits*. 6 vols. Paris: Maisonneuve et Cie, 1879-88. Copies of the translation are in the Burton Historical Collection (Detroit Public Library); the Library of Michigan (Lansing); and the University of Chicago.

Munro, William Bennett. *The Seignorial System in Canada: A Study in French Colonial Policy*. New York: Longmans, Green and Co., 1907.

Pariseau, Jean. "Le Mercier (Mercier), François-Marc-Antoine." *Dictionary of Canadian Biography*, 4:458-61.

Pease, Theodore Calvin, and Ernestine Jenison, eds. *Collections of the Illinois State Historical Library*. 38 vols. Springfield: Illinois State Historical Library, 1903-75.

Pelletier, Jean-Guy. "Coulon de Villiers, Nicolas-Antoine." *Dictionary of Canadian Biography*, 2:156.

Peyser, Joseph L. "The Chickasaw Wars of 1736 and 1740: French Military Drawings and Plans Document the Struggle for the Lower Mississippi." *The Journal of Mississippi History* 44, no. 1 (February 1982): 1-25.

_____."The Fall and Rise of Thérèse Catin: A Portrait from Indiana's French and Canadian History." *Indiana Magazine of History* 91, no. 4 (December 1995): 378-79.

_____. *Jacques Legardeur de Saint-Pierre: Officer, Gentleman, Entrepreneur.* East Lansing/Mackinac Island: Michigan State University Press/Mackinac State Historic Parks, 1996.

_____. *Letters from New France: The Upper Country 1686-1783.* Urbana: University of Illinois Press, 1992.

Pouchot, Pierre. *Memoirs on the Late War in North America between France and England,* edited by Brian Leigh Dunnigan and translated by Michael Cardy. Youngstown, N.Y.: Old Fort Niagara Publications, 1994.

Pritchard, James. *Anatomy of a Naval Disaster: The 1746 French Expedition to North America.* Montreal & Kingston: McGill-Queen's University Press, 1995.

Richter, Daniel K. *The Ordeal of the Longhouse: The Peoples of the Iroquois League in the Era of European Colonization.* Chapel Hill: University of North Carolina Press, 1992.

Robert, Paul. *Dictionnaire alphabétique et analogique de la langue française.* 6 vols. Paris: Société du Nouveau Littré, 1960-64.

_____. *Le Petit Robert: Dictionnaire alphabétique & analogique de la langue française.* Paris: Société du Nouveau Littré, 1978.

Ross, Lester A. *Archaeological Metrology: English, French, American and Canadian Systems of Weights and Measures for North American Archaeology.* History and Archaeology Series, No. 68. Hull, Canada: Canadian Government Publishing Center, Supply and Services Canada, 1983.

Roy, Pierre-Georges. "Charles, Chevalier de Raymond." *Bulletin des recherches historiques,* 54:165-66.

Severance, Frank H. *An Old Frontier of France: The Niagara Region and Adjacent Lakes under French Control.* 2 vols. New York: Dodd, Mead and Co., 1917.

Thwaites, Reuben G., ed. *Jesuit Relations and Allied Documents.* 73 vols. Cleveland: Burrows Brothers, 1896-1901.

Tousignant, Pierre, and Madeleine Dionne-Tousignant. "La Corne, Luc de." *Dictionary of Canadian Biography,* 4:425-28.

Trap, Paul. "Mouet de Langlade, Charles-Michel." *Dictionary of Canadian Biography,* 4:563-64.

Trubowitz, Neal L. "Native Americans and French on the Central Wabash." In *Calumet & Fleur-de-Lys: Archaeology of Indian and French Contact in the Midcontinent,* edited by John A. Walthall and Thomas E. Emerson, 241-64. Washington, D.C.: Smithsonian Institution, 1992.

Trudel, Marcel. *Initiation à la Nouvelle-France.* Montreal: Les éditions HRW ltée, 1971.

Usner, Daniel H. Jr. *Indians, Settlers, & Slaves in a Frontier Exchange Economy: The Lower Mississippi Valley before 1783*. Chapel Hill: University of North Carolina Press, 1992.

Walthall, John A., and Thomas E. Emerson, eds. *Calumet & Fleur-de-Lys: Archaeology of Indian and French Contact in the Midcontinent*. Washington, D.C.: Smithsonian Institution, 1992.

Waselkov, Gregory A. "French Colonial Trade in the Upper Creek Country." In *Calumet & Fleur-de-Lys: Archaeology of Indian and French Contact in the Midcontinent*, edited by John A. Walthall and Thomas E. Emerson, 35-53. Washington, D.C.: Smithsonian Institution, 1992.

Washington, George. *The Journal of Major George Washington*, 1754; facsimile ed. Williamsburg: Colonial Williamsburg Foundation, 1959.

White, Richard. *The Middle Ground: Indians, Empires, and Republics in the Great Lakes Region*. Cambridge: Cambridge University Press, 1991.

Zoltvany, Yves F. "Gaultier de Varennes et de La Vérendrye, Pierre." *Dictionary of Canadian Biography*, 3:246-54.

_____. "La Porte de Louvigny, Louis de." *Dictionary of Canadian Biography*, 2:345-47.

_____. *The French Tradition in America*. Columbia: University of South Carolina Press, 1969.

INTERVIEWS

Dunnigan, Brian Leigh. Telephone interview. 18 December 1996.

Edmunds, R. David. Telephone interview. 22 January 1995.

INDEX

Hudson Bay

Fort La Jonquière

Fort Paskoya 2

Cedar Lake

Saskatchewan

Western Sea Posts

Fort Bourbon 2

Lake Winnipegosis

Lake Winnipeg

Fort Dauphin

Lake Manitoba

Fort La Reine

Fort Maurepas 2

Winnipeg

Lake of the Woods

Lake Nipigon

Fort Rouge

Fort Saint-Charles

Fort St. Pierre

Rainy Lake

Kaministiquia (Thunder Bay)

Nipigon

Grand Portage

Michipicote

Missouri

Lake Superior

Lake Itasca

Sandy Lake

St. Louis

Chagouamigon (La Pointe)

St. Croix

Sau

Fort Michi

Lake Michigan

Minnesota

Mississippi

Wisconsin

Fort La Baye (Green Bay)

Lake Winnebago

Muskegon

Sag.

North Platte

South Platte

Platte

Des Moines

Rock

Illinois

Fort St. Joseph

Kankakee

St. Joseph

Pic

Vermilion

Fort Ouiatanon (West Lafayette)

Missouri

Kaskaskia

Cahokia

Vincennes

Wabash

Ohio

Arkansas

Fort Chartres (Prairie du Rocher)

Kaskaskia

Mississippi

cartography by
Department of Geography
Michigan State University